DISPLAY PILOT
FLYING THE RAF's COMBAT AIRCRAFT

DISPLAY PILOT
FLYING THE RAF's COMBAT AIRCRAFT

Flight Lieutenant Rob Lea

OSPREY
AEROSPACE

ACKNOWLEDGEMENTS

My grateful thanks to Tony Holmes, who wrote the Shuttleworth chapter, provided captions for the photographs and was instrumental in producing, publishing and editing the book. I would also like to acknowledge the help of the following individuals; 'Jac Spratt', Mick and the 'Typing Ladies'; Sqn Ldr Steve Cockram and Flt Lt Eddie Middleton (No II(AC) Sqn); Flt Lts Jerry Goatham and Paul Brown (No 56(R) Sqn); Flt Lt Geraint Herbert (Standards Flight RAF Valley); Flt Lt Phil Jones (No 3 FTS); Flt Lts Neil Benson and Gary Davies (No 208 Sqn); Sqn Ldr Roy Bouch and Flt Lts Keith Harding and Tony Graves (No 42(R) Sqn); Sqn Ldr Don MacIntosh and Flt Lt Nigel Watson (No 57(R) Sqn); Flt Lt Andy Cubin (No 16(R) Sqn); and Flt Lts Adrian Pickard and Brian Little.

Bronica Co Ltd also deserve a special mention for the provision of photographic equipment, and last, but by no means least, a big 'thank you' to my wife Suzanne for performing the editorial duties, as well as supporting me throughout the season.

The editor wishes to thank the following photographers for supplying extra material for this volume; John Dibbs, David Davies/Air Portraits, Geoff Lee, Mike Stroud, Cliff Knox, Duncan Cubitt, John Durston and C J Wallace. Tim Senior at *Aerospace Publishing* and Mike Badrocke also deserve a mention for their contributions, as does the legendary Bill Bedford for his foreword. Thank you also to T Malcolm English and *Air International* for allowing us to reproduce the author's piece on display work-ups, featured in chapter two, and similarly to Zoe Schofield, editor of *Air Display International*, for granting us permission to use both the Hercules article, written by Andy Evans, and the Tornado F.3 piece. Finally, thanks to Bryan Lewis at Shuttleworth for the airfield access.

First published in Great Britain in 1994
by Osprey, an imprint of Reed Consumer Books Limited
Michelin House, 81 Fulham Road, London SW3 6RB
and Auckland, Melbourne, Singapore and Toronto

ISBN 1 85532 445 8

Edited by Tony Holmes
Production Controller Alison Myer
Page Design by Jim Miller,
Bridgewater Design, Hove, East Sussex

Printed in Hong Kong

ABOVE: RAF Wittering's 'engineer section' on an away day! Perched precariously on the panels that cover the accessory equipment gearbox, Cpl Bassett gets to grips with a wiring problem that had manifested itself in the 'spare' jet which had partnered Rob Lea to the Isle of Man for the Jurby Air Show on 8 August 1993. Having successfully completed the display on the Sunday, Rob and his No 2, Flt Lt Spike Jepson, had departed Ronaldsway Airport on Monday morning and headed south for Wittering. Shortly after take-off, Jepson (himself an ex-Harrier display pilot who is now flying with the Red Arrows) had a fire caption indicator flash on his BIT panel. Both Harriers immediately returned to the Isle of Man, as it was the nearest airfield, and performed a precautionary landing. The engineering support team that had accompanied the jets to the display was still at Ronaldsway, and led by Pegasus specialist Cpl Bassett, they soon found the fault – a break in the fire warning wire was causing spurious indications within the cockpit. The small team quickly rectified the glitch, enabling the jets to fly back as a pair to Wittering by the afternoon

TITLE PAGES: The 1993 airshow season saw the Harrier GR.7 join the GR.5 as the V/STOL demonstrator on the display circuit, the fully updated jets being delivered directly to Wittering following their reworking by British Aerospace. Climbing away from Cambridgeshire at the beginning of a transit flight, this immaculate aircraft boasts a pair of 250 gal tanks beneath its composite wings *(Photo by John Dibbs)*

CONTENTS

FOREWORD

'LE BOURGET tower, this is Display 103 requesting permission to join your circuit for practice demonstration in Harrier.'

The instantaneous response was, 'Bill, this is Georges. The airfield is yours!' Georges Veillot was an old and trusted friend who understood the strange behaviour of the British, and the eccentricity of Chief Test Pilots – he was the Chief of Air Traffic Control at the 1967 Paris Le Bourget aviation salon.

His warm welcome on my arrival from Dunsfold aerodrome, combined both with the Hawker Experimental Department's painstaking preparation of my Harrier and my airshow practice back in England, stimulated and inspired my confidence as I put the jet through its paces. The big crowd and the world media watched with respect and anticipation, doubtless remembering my spectacular arrival at Le Bourget in 1963 with Hawker P.1127 XP831 when, on the final Sunday, it crashed ignominiously on the special reinforced concrete platform designed for our rival, the multi-engined Dassault Balzac (Mirage IIIV forerunner).

A lethal, undemanded and massive movement of the vectored thrust in the P.1127 had it one moment behaving normally at 50 ft, and then the next plummeting earthwards totally out of control to scatter aviation scrap metal hither and thither. Nine months later I tested XP831 with effective modifications to ensure that the engine exhaust nozzles (thrust vectored) always remained in the position last selected!

Thirty years on Flt Lt Rob Lea of the RAF occupies the 'hot seat' as No 1 Harrier demonstration pilot, with the challenge and responsibility that it carries. 1994 will be his second year in this capacity, and I join the readers of this volume in wishing him continued success. Additionally, and most importantly, Rob is also required to play a full role instructing with the Harrier Operational Conversion Unit. He is now a most experienced Harrier demonstration pilot who has enhanced the reputation of the RAF, the Harrier and his home station of RAF Wittering.

Rob's brilliant and imaginative displays not only highlight the big advances made in the V/STOL handling qualities of the Harrier GR.5/7 family of aircraft, but they also illustrate the greatly improved manoeuvrability resultant upon the aircraft's larger wing, which incorporates some unique aerodynamic characteristics.

The aim of demonstration flying is to promote the product and to enhance the prestige of the service and/or the manufacturer by a safe, stimulating display. Well do I remember an enthusiastic ex-RAF fighter pilot come Hawker sales executive, with a black patch over one eye, being present whilst a desperately dull Harrier display was being carried out overhead at Dunsfold. When asked by the groundcrew chief when to tow the aircraft back to the hangar, he said two things; 'Ignore it and let it slink back when no-one is looking, and remind me to bring a second black patch when that so and so is so called display flying!'

It is essential to have a pilot who is instinctively attracted to, and at home with, demonstration flying. Then comes the necessary concentration, discipline and constant practice, along with the willingness to accept constructive criticism from a respected ground observer.

To avoid pitfalls, an important element is (except in an emergency) to stick with concentrated determination to the practised format and adhere to one's own strict professional code. You have to aim for the narrow compromise between a wet and uninspiring display and an edge of the envelope rodeo show.

The low-level demonstration arena is one of the most demanding and hostile environments in which the pilot operates. It has indeed killed far too many pilots, and only by the grace of God am I here to write this foreword. The margin for error is small, and the pilot is flying close to the handling and performance limits in a competitive environment.

My 1967 Harrier display at Le Bourget was over and Georges Veillot arranged for me to return to the UK immediately the flying programme ended. I was lined up on the main runway ready to go when the *Patrouille de France* aerobatic team with its nine Fouga Magisters did a spectacular, but fairly low, smoking bomb burst formation break which left the jets pointing vertically at the ground. One pilot failed to pull out and the aircraft smashed into the ground 300 metres in front of me, exploding in a brilliant orange fireball. Sadly, the pilot, Captain Duthoit was killed instantly. I stayed silent and sad in my cockpit, not wishing to worry ATC. An unperturbed sparrow flew past my windscreen, giving me an uncaring glance.

In this book Rob Lea writes of the meticulous care and preparation that goes into the exacting task of display flying, procedures that I whole heartedly endorse. These are the pilot's life insurance policy. CONCENTRATE, and remember that no matter how brilliant you think you are, each of us is but a fallible human being – I know from bitter experience after nearly killing myself in a Hunter spinning demonstration in 1959 through failing to reset the altimeter. I was Hawker's Chief Test Pilot at the time, and I only confessed to it 18 years later when I saw so many friends and colleagues kill themselves in demonstration flying.

I have made it my crusade, not as the 'Pope of Aviation' but as a flying 'sinner', to alert people to the inherent dangers of displaying aircraft of any type incorrectly. A Japanese saying sums it up perfectly; 'Even a monkey can fall from a tree!'

Bill Bedford

A W (Bill) Bedford OBE, AFC, FRAeS
Hawker Experimental Test Pilot then Chief Test Pilot 1951-1967
(Carried out first flights on P.1127, Kestrel and Harrier)

24th December 1993

LEFT: V/STOL display flying all started with this humble individual making the first tentative (and tethered) hops in the P.1127 prototype at Dunsfold airfield on 21 October 1960. By the time Hawker's Chief Test Pilot, Bill Bedford, was photographed standing alongside Kestrel XS690 at the 1965 Paris Airshow, the concept of the V/STOL combat aircraft had almost reached tangible reality, with the introduction of the Harrier GR.1 into RAF service less than four years later. Hawkers had to borrow this jet from the Kestrel Evaluation Squadron at RAF West Raynham, in Norfolk, as they couldn't furnish Bill with a suitable aircraft from their own stocks. After three days of typically impressive airshow flying by Hawker's number one pilot at Le Bourget, Bill ferried the jet back to the UK intact – at the previous Salon two years earlier, Bill's P.1127 had made a rather heavy landing following a technical malfunction which had caused the engine nozzles to rotate aft independently of the pilot's control inputs! *(Photo by Hawker Siddeley Avaition Manchester via Bill Bedford)*

AUTOBIOGRAPHY

I AM not one of those people who's been desperate to fly ever since being 'knee-high to a grasshopper'. I wanted to be a Marine Biologist. I marvelled at the exploits of Jaques Cousteau and despite living within a mile of RAF Woodvale, I barely noticed the daily groan of Bulldog and Chipmunk engines overhead.

It was not until I was accepted to study Marine Biology at Liverpool University that my mind opened to the world of flying. I remember thumbing through the University's prospectus in the summer, to see what clubs were on offer and seeing 'Free flying. No obligation. Apply now to Liverpool University Air Squadron'.

It seemed too good to be true. Intrigued, I visited RAF Woodvale, home of the University's Air Squadron (UAS), and was welcomed by the Administrative Officer, Tony Nadden. After a guided tour, he explained that the squadron would be interviewing potential members during the first weeks of term – 'we'll see you there!', were his parting words to me.

The UAS interviews followed roughly the same format that I was to experience at the Officer and Aircrew Selection Centre at Biggin Hill three years later. Informal questions about family history and hobbies, and then more probing questions concerning motivation, the RAF and general service knowledge. On the latter subject I knew painfully little – I could not identify the air-

ABOVE: An embroiderer's nightmare, the highly detailed Euro-Nato Joint Jet Pilot Training (ENJJPT) crest is worn by all students and Instructors involved in this long-running programme. The RAF sends six pilots a year to ENJJPT primarily as a political committment to its NATO allies – the air force is more than happy with its own Training Command structure. Some member countries like Germany do not possess their own basic training system, however, and rely on ENJJPT to churn out their future aircrew

BELOW: A veritable rogue's gallery pose for their induction photograph at the now-closed Officer and Aircrew Selection Centre at Biggin Hill in December 1983. 'B1', alias Lars Smith, graduated to fly Tornado GR.1s, including seeing combat in the Gulf, and is now a QFI at a University Air Squadron; 'B2', Phil O'dell went on to Buccaneers and now instructs on Hawks at RAF Valley; 'B3' is occasionally spotted around the 'bazaars' in a Harrier GR.5 or 7; and 'B4', Mike Lumb, is currently serving as a Tornado GR.1 navigator. 'B6' 'Josh' Joship was unsuccessful in his application to join the RAF, and the fate of 'B5' Rob Jones is unknown

LEFT: Practising formation flying over 'the Moss', to the east of RAF Woodvale, in Lancashire, Rob sticks close to a fellow Liverpool University Air Squadron (UAS) Bulldog T.2 in late 1982. The syllabus within the UAS is very similar to that followed by the RAF's basic flying training squadrons, giving ab initio pilots a taste of aerobatics, instrument flying, low-level navigation and formation flying. Rob's UAS days gave him a love of flying that has remained with him ever since

craft pictured on the walls, and it must have been all too obvious that I had only very recently entertained the notion of joining the UAS. Nevertheless, a few weeks later I was overjoyed to hear that I had been accepted.

My first flight in a Bulldog was a very exciting experience, and I was fortunate enough to see my home town of Southport as I'd never seen it before, with amazing views of the Lake District to the north and Wales to the south. However, I was rather shocked on my second trip when I realised that flying was not just a matter of taking in the scenery – there was far too much else to do!

The first six months of flying were hard work. It was a very alien environment, and I didn't really understand what I was trying to achieve. It was not until the first summer camp, when the squadron detached to RAF Leuchars, in Scotland, for an entire month during the University stand-down, that I was able to fly on a regular basis. It was as though a light had been switched on. I was enjoying the flying and at last began to develop a feel for the aircraft. During the following year, as I progressed onto aerobatics, low flying and formation work, my love of flying grew, and when not studying at Liverpool, I spent every available moment at Woodvale.

For the third and final year of my degree, I moved from Liverpool to the Port Erin Marine Laboratory, situated at the southern tip of the Isle of Man. Here, I would put into practice the theory of my previous two years. It was to be an idyllic time, living in a student bungalow in the picturesque village of Port Erin and walking along the beach to work at what must be the most ideally situated marine laboratory in Europe. When not in the field centre, I would be 'work-diving' in the bay, or further afield from one of the laboratory's diving boats. Life could hardly have been better, apart from the flying – or lack of it. My meagre grant would not allow trips to the 'mainland' and so I had to drop any hopes of flying for the year. This was a sobering experience. I missed it immensely and this led me to the conclusion that I had to make flying my career. I applied to join the RAF in December 1983 and was accepted three months later.

My life in the RAF proper initially followed the conventional path, beginning with 18 weeks at the Department of Initial Officer Training at Cranwell. I was then fortunate enough to be sent to the Euro NATO Joint Jet Pilot Training Programme (ENJJPT) at Sheppard Air Force Base, Texas, instead of following the normal route through one of the three basic flying training schools in the UK.

Six RAF student pilots embark on the 14-month programme every year, joining a class of

ABOVE: The temperature is regularly in the mid-90s at Sheppard AFB, the Texas home of the ENJJPT scheme, and students tend to work themselves into a sweat during their first solo flight in a Cessna T-37, so a dunk in the base 'pool' is a must after a tense sortie. Graciously helped in by fellow 86-04 classmates Frank Kiesel from Germany and Bob Griffin from America, Rob practices his water survival techniques for the camera. 'I remember that the bottom of the pool was littered with dead insects as the water was never cleaned from one year to the next', he exclaimed – ideal research material for a marine biologist one would have thought!

30 which is made up of students from 12 other NATO countries. Similarly, the instructors also hail from a variety of nations, making the course truly Euro-NATO. I joined the romantically titled '86-04' class (the name related to our proposed graduation date of April 1986). Flying began on the Cessna T-37, an aircraft that resembles the RAF's late-lamented Jet Provost, and whose performance lay somewhere between that of the JP3 and 5. A noisy, hot and uncomfortable aircraft, the T-37 was not popular with the students, but served as a suitable platform for learning jet handling and for working through the various basic flying phases.

After six months, and 130 flying hours, we progressed onto the Northrop T-38 Talon. The twin-afterburning T-38, with its tandem seating, hydraulic controls and supersonic performance, felt and looked like a fighter. Capable of cruising at speeds in excess of 600 kts, sustaining 5g turns and flying a whole host of new aerobatic manoeuvres, the Talon was undoubtedly a step in the

ABOVE: Glad to see the back of the T-37, Rob moved onto the 'sportiest' American trainer of the past 30 years, the Northrop T-38 Talon. Checking to see that both General Electric J85-GE-6 turbojet engines are correctly installed and the exhaust nozzles are free of damage, a young Flg Off Lea commences the pre-flight walk-around of his aircraft prior to strapping in. Rob is wearing a USAF-style flying suit adorned with an RAF rank tab

right direction. The syllabus also moved forward in keeping with the aircraft's performance, with ever more complex sorties including four-ship tactical formations and longer range cross-counties being undertaken.

By this stage, I had flown with all sorts of instructors including Germans, Greeks, Italians, Americans and Danes. Many of these pilots, although enjoying their time in the US, were quite critical of the 'American way of doing things', stating that the emphasis placed upon procedural flying tended to produce students who lacked flexibility and were not practised at using their initiative. With hindsight, although the Americans could be criticised for sticking to their procedures, and perhaps for over-emphasising instrument and formation flying to the detriment of low-level navigation, there would be plenty of opportunity to practice these neglected skills later, and with over 200 training aircraft flying from the same base on two parallel runways every day, a high degree of control was needed in order to prevent mayhem.

By the end of the course, I had accrued over 260 flying hours, travelled extensively throughout America and grown to know a small number of valued friends from a variety of backgrounds. At the graduation ceremony we were awarded both USAF and RAF wings, and class members were told of their future assignments. For us, there were no surprises – we had known from the beginning that if successful, we would be returning to RAF Valley to fly a conversion course on the Hawk. However, for the rest of the course, particularly the Americans, this was the moment critique when they would find out whether they had achieved their 'dream shot'. Most of our class mates had no reason to be disappointed, nine receiving plum F-15 slots and four the F-16.

Anglesey was something of a change after the hot, featureless plains of Texas, although a number of similarities spring to mind! As we joined our course, which consisted of students from Cranwell, Linton-on-Ouse and Church Fenton, we felt rather conscious of our newly acquired wings, for in the RAF system, they are not awarded until after completion of the Valley course (or at Finninly/Shawbury for multi-engine/helicopter pilots). However, we need not have worried, as our course mates readily accepted us.

My primary instructor was an exchange officer from the Navy. I found this situation rather ironic, for having been taught by Germans and Danes, on returning to the folds of the RAF, I was now being taught by the 'Senior Service'! Still, the instruction was no less sound, and I very much enjoyed flying the Hawk. With its excellent

view, ergonomically-designed cockpit and superb handling characteristics, the jet was popular with everyone. Although it lacked the supersonic performance of the T-38, the Hawk was capable of high rates of turn and could loop inside 4000 ft; by comparison, the Talon struggled tp perform a similar manoeuvre within 10,000 ft! Of course, high turn-rates are accompanied by high g-forces, and these took a little getting used to.

For the initial conversion course, we were allocated fewer hours than our class mates as our T-38 experience was expected to ease our transition. However, Valley was by no means an attendance course, many ENJJPT students having been chopped in years gone by due to poor low-level navigation skills, or through failing to adjust to UK procedures.

By the end of the six-month course, we had faired reasonably well. Eleven of us had started it and only one had been re-streamed onto multi-engines, whilst another, who suffered badly from

ABOVE: Looking every inch the fast jet pilot, Rob proudly strikes a pose moments before climbing aboard 'his' jet. The backdrop for this shot was Talon 69-7077, the youngest airframe then attached to the 90th FTS within the 80th FTW. As well as having to endure temperatures not usually experienced by Lancastrians, and a flightline rather larger than that at Woodvale, Rob's task was made even harder by the fact that all crews had to walk out to their T-38s wearing a parachute, as, unlike most other modern trainers, the aircraft's elderly ejection seat was not integrally fitted with such a device

ABOVE: The culmination of four years of hard work within Support and Strike Command – Flt Lt Lea awaits the signal to 'scramble' from his 'hide' somewhere in Denmark during a NATO exercise in 1988. Prior to being posted to No 1(F) Sqn, Rob first spent six months with the Harrier Operational Conversion Unit learning the unique art of V/STOL flying. As part of Allied Command Europe's Mobile Force (Air), No 1(F) Sqn spends several weeks away every year, usually in the Scandinavian region, deployed in the field and operating from hides (in the past 12 months the unit has been helping enforce the United Nations 'no fly zone' in Iraq, operating from bases in Turkey). Firmly strapped in and with his GR.3 connected to a Houchin for rapid engine spool-up, Rob is receiving target and routing information, via a land-line, through his head set. Whilst he plans his next sortie from within the cockpit, the 'hide' team of engineers service the Harrier, reloading fuel and weapons in time for the next sortie. The netting which covers the 'hide' is very effective in preventing the GR.3 from being spotted by 'enemy' aircraft flying reconnaissance sorties over the area

ABOVE: Following the completion of his training on Hawks, Rob was posted to Harriers, but before arriving at Wittering he first spent a week at Shawbury with No 2 FTS gaining experience in vertical take-off and hovering techniques. Equipped with Gazelle HT.2s and 3s, the unit was described by Rob as the 'best kept secret in the RAF', the pilot concentrating purely on flying the helicopter, rather than learning about its systems. All sorties are performed with an instructor in the right-hand seat, and due to the responsiveness and light weight of the Gazelle, it is not too difficult to master

air-sickness, was sent on the aircrew desensitisation course at the institute of Aviation Medicine, Farnborough. For the remainder, fast jet training would continue at either Brawdy, in South Wales, or Chivenor, in North Devon.

I was posted to the Tactical Weapons Unit at Chivenor, and as my course did not immediately follow our Valley graduation, I was temporarily attached to No 10 Air Experience Flight at RAF Woodvale. Two mellow, fulfilling, months followed in which I flew Air Cadets on air experience and familiarisation trips, whilst attempting to get to grips with the Chipmunk. A relatively forgiving aircraft in the air, the Chipmunk was a devil to land – at least to land on three wheels. This was my first experience of tail-draggers, and it proved quite challenging. It was also the first time in my Air Force career that my performance had not been scrutinised with the aid of a micro-

scope, and I found that I was able to relax and simply enjoy flying for flying's sake.

My arrival at Chivenor was less auspicious than I had planned. Although I had survived many a drive along the notoriously dangerous A5 pass whilst travelling to Valley, the supposedly routine journey to Chivenor was not so successful. Debris on the roadside caused a simultaneous blowout on both near side tyres, slewing the car uncontrollably off the road. By the time I had graunched to a halt, with the help of a 'natural stone' wall, it was quite obvious that for this car, the war was over. A few hours later, I was delivered to the front of the Officers' Mess aboard an AA recovery vehicle, with the wreckage of my car, sitting on the rear. Not realising that on this particular evening, Chivenor was holding its Christmas Draw celebrations, it was unfortunate for me that the first person that I bumped into was the

Station Commander with a guest on each arm, who, in no uncertain terms, suggested I remove my heap from his sight.

Chivenor had a refreshingly different atmosphere from all of the bases that I had so far experienced. The aircraft had swapped their red and white training colours for tactical paint schemes, and they carried guns, Sidewinder missiles and practice bombs – we had moved from 'Support' to 'Strike' Command. At our arrival briefing, it was made clear that we would no longer be treated with kid gloves. We had earned our wings and were expected to perform accordingly. The instructors were not there to teach us how to fly – that was taken as read. Here we would learn how to operate the aircraft.

The course began with tactical formation work, and quickly progressed onto air-to-air gunsight training. Before long we were firing the cannon and dropping bombs on the range. The pace of life was fairly frantic as there were a number of new skills to be mastered in a short period of time. Nevertheless, as the end of the course neared, we were beginning to get to grips with the basic concepts associated with air combat, evasion and low level attack profiles.

At this stage, we were asked to submit a list of our preferred aircraft types for the future. Nick-named 'dream-sheets' for obvious reasons, we knew that these lists provided only one of many inputs influencing out next posting, the major factors being performance on the course and availability of slots. At the time the outcome seemed to take on life and death proportions, tension reaching fever pitch as 'D-Day' approached. Now I could see why the Americans had been so excited 14 months earlier. I was desperate to fly Harriers and could hardly believe my ears when told that I had been posted to RAF Wittering.

With only three to four courses a year, it was obvious that I would have a short hold before starting. At last my Marine Biological background would prove useful.

I was detached to Gibraltar to teach diving at the Joint Services Diving Centre. Very closely resembling a holiday, my stay in the Mediterranean was all too quickly over, and I soon returned to the UK, a little more tanned than when I had left, to commence lead-in training. This consisted of a week of helicopter flying at Shawbury, followed by a few days penance at the Aviation-Medical Training Centre, in North Luffenham. The course at Shawbury is undoubtedly one of the RAF's best kept secrets. There are

ABOVE: Called into action by an Army platoon pinned down by elements of 'red force', Rob taxies out from his 'hide' along a disused road prior to positioning himself for take-off. Up to six sorties a day are flown whilst on exercise, and they consist primarily of short close air support missions of 30 minutes duration. Upon returning to the site, the Harrier pilot would perform a vertical landing onto a steel 'mexe pad', the jet then being manually pushed back into its hide

no checks to learn, systems to study, or emergencies to worry about, just hours of entertainment learning to take-off, hover and land the Gazelle in the picturesque countryside surrounding Shrewsbury.

Armed with our newly acquired hovering skills, we began the six-month Harrier conversion course which I've described in full detail in chapter five.

From the Operational Conversion Unit, I was posted a few hundred yards 'down the road' to No 1(Fighter) Sqn, remaining at Wittering. Within a week of my arrival, I was flying over the majestic snow-covered mountains of Norway on a squadron deployment to Bardufoss. This was just one of a number of theatres in which the unit exercised. Germany, Denmark, Sardinia and Belize (in Central America) also saw our regular visits as individuals practised the variety of roles associated with each of the different theatres. Maritime work on the carrier, field deployments in Europe and Winter operations north of the Arctic Circle all added to the range of sorties, ensuring that life was anything but routine.

When at home, I continued working towards combat ready status, and later on for my air combat leader, pairs leader and eventually 'fours' leader tickets.

In January 1989, No 1(F) Sqn introduced the Harrier force to the GR.5, becoming the first unit to convert from the GR.3 within the RAF. Never before had a change of aircraft mark concealed such an enormous improvement in capability. A complete re-design had produced an aircraft with nearly double the range, twice the payload, greatly improved rates of turn and state of the art avionics. All these features combined to make the GR.5 an enormous hit, and for the next 15 months I enjoyed exercising the RAF 's latest aircraft in the roles and theatres inherited from the GR.3.

In the spring of 1990, I left the Harrier and was posted to the Central Flying School at RAF Scampton (near Lincoln) to embark upon a flying instructors' course. Upon my graduation six months later, I moved south to RAF Cranwell as a qualified flying instructor on the Jet Provost. As I had not previously experienced the RAF's basic flying training system, this was something of a novelty for me, and it was interesting to witness life on the other side of the student/instructor fence.

A few months later, the Tucano arrived at Cranwell. At the time this was quite a controversial change, as the Shorts turboprop seemed to lack some of the jet-like handling characteristics for which it had been purchased. However, the aircraft was instantly popular with the

ABOVE: In late November 1988 No 1(F) Sqn became the first frontline RAF unit to receive GR.5s. Prior to taking the jet abroad on exercise the 'Fighting First' conducted field deployments for up to a week in simulated sites along the western edge of its Wittering base. Sitting in his 'hide' listening to a tasking message that includes details of the mission target, type of weapon required and routing points, Rob is poised with chinagraphs at the ready to mark these details on the 'fablon' map perched on his lap. Following a successful spell with the unit, Rob was posted to the Central Flying School at RAF Scampton to be trained as a QFI. Upon graduation he was posted to RAF Cranwell and No 3 FTS, where he flew Jet Provost T.5As and Tucano T.1s. In February 1992 he returned to No 233 OCU and the Harrier

students, and it was gradually accepted as the new way ahead in the basic flying training system.

My stay at Cranwell was shorter than I had expected. In February 1992, just 17 months after my arrival, I was posted back to Wittering, this time to serve as an instructor on the Harrier Operational Conversion Unit.

As I later discovered, this move was to provide me with the opportunity of becoming the Harrier Display Pilot.

HARRIER TAKES A BOW

'CONGRATULATIONS Rob. You're going to be next year's Harrier display pilot', said the boss as we walked down the stairs to the operations room. 'That is assuming the Air Officer Commanding (AOC) gives his approval', he added wryly. The month was December, and already preparations for next year's airshow season were under way.

The thought of displaying the Harrier at the string of events around Britain, and indeed in Europe, was very exciting, but it was also quite a daunting task, for as well as being display pilot, I was also required to play a full role instructing on the Harrier Operational Conversion Unit at Wittering. It would be a very busy six months. Ever since my UAS experiences at Liverpool, the idea of displaying an aircraft had greatly appealed. Even in those early days, it was not any illusions of glory or cheering crowds that inspired me, rather the thought of flying a jet close to its limits in the demanding environment of a low-level display.

BELOW LEFT: Twenty years ago Harrier GR.1 display pilots practised their routines on a quiet afternoon at altitude above Wittering, working up their manoeuvres over a series of flights into a tight sequences of turns, climbs, high speed runs and hovers. They would perhaps discuss their proposed routine with former display pilots still on the squadron, making notes and mentally rehearsing their sequences. However, at the end of the day, when the pilot wrung his Harrier out at the edge of its performance envelope for the very first time, no amount of mental rehearsal could have totally prepared him for the stresses and strains of that inaugural flight. Today's display pilot can save himself a lot of anxiety, and the taxpayer several thousand pounds, by systematically 'flying' his routine within Wittering's state-of-the-art Link-Miles Ltd GR.5 simulator. By the time Rob first took to the skies for real in late January 1993, he had flown the basis of his full display many times over in the simulator. In this dramatic view, photographed within the visual dome of the system, Rob is practising his 400-kt inverted pass which he performs following a half-Cuban positioning manoeuvre. Due to oil and fuel considerations, the Harrier GR.5/7's period of inversion is limited to 15 seconds

Having established that I was now in the displaying business, I needed to prepare for the coming season. But where to begin? Obviously, the flying sequence merited immediate consideration. Each year the pilot is given a free reign to design his own display, but the sequence cannot be flown below 5000 ft (1524 m) until it has been scrutinised and approved by a number of individuals, including the squadron boss, station commander, a team at group headquarters and ultimately the AOC.

This is not a problem for most fast jet pilots, for they can develop their display aloft and when cleared, gradually bring it down to crowd-pleasing heights. Unfortunately the Harrier doesn't lend itself to this treatment. As anyone who's seen the Harrier display knows, hovering and jet-borne flight form an integral part of the show, and yet contrary to popular belief, the Harrier cannot hover at 5000 ft (1524 m), preventing practise aloft. Herein lies the paradox. How can you design a sequence without practical experimentation?

In order to solve this problem, I turned to the recently completed GR.5 simulator at Wittering. It was fortunate that the simulator was serviceable for until recently, all simulator training had been carried out at one of two US Marine Corps bases – Yuma in Arizona and Cherry Point in North Carolina – and in these days of financial accountability, an overseas visit for display design was out of the question.

The Wittering GR.5 simulator was built by Link-Miles Ltd, the contract that was awarded to the company in December 1986 covering the production of two flight simulators; one at Wittering, and a second that was delivered to RAF Laarbruch in late 1993. The Wittering simulator comprises a GR.5 cockpit, located within a visual dome. The simulator's visual projectors are all located within the dome, which is

itself mounted on a motion system that accurately produces the full range of flight-induced motion responses. The computers and hardware needed to drive and operate the simulator are located in an adjacent building, together with the training management system that comprises an instructors' operating station (resembling the flight deck of the *Starship Enterprise*) and a remote debriefing facility. Two simulator instructors control operations and monitor pilot performance.

LEFT: Of all the RAF's display aircraft, the Harrier is perhaps best equipped ergonomically for airshow work, its cockpit being spacious and well laid out. A large Smiths Industries SU-128/A glass head-up display (HUD), linked with a CP-1450/A display computer manufactured by the same company, help the pilot keep in full control of his aircraft. At a glance Rob has all the relevant data on the physical state of the jet, as well as the flight parameters he is currently controlling like speed, height, attitude and, of course, heading. Finally, to top it all, the Harrier GR.7 is blessed with one of the largest areas of canopy fitted to any modern combat aircraft, giving the pilot commanding views around a full 360° axis – a marked improvement over the GR.3, in which the pilot cannot even see over his own wings!

1993 Harrier GR.7 Display

MANOEUVRE A

LEFT: Short take-off, 150° climbing turn and wing-under

The main innovation of the simulator is the visual system, developed and built in the US. To provide a highly detailed visual scene over the entire dome surface would be prohibitively expensive in terms of computing power. To overcome this problem, two projectors are used – one projects a low detail scene over the entire dome surface and the other projects a circular high detail scene of approximately 3 ft (1 m) diameter, merged into the low detail scene. This high detail scene precisely follows the eye movement of the pilot, and so is always at the point where he is looking. The pilot therefore only sees the high detail scene and is fooled into thinking that this continues into his peripheral vision.

A computer-generated visual database provides the scenes for the pilot. Using the database workstation, co-located with the simulator, visual scenes can be generated from satellite data, thus providing images of anywhere in the world. Before strapping into the simulator, the specially-designed £100,000 helmet with mounted camera needs to be precisely fitted and aligned. Once in the cockpit, an eye-slaving calibration exercise is carried out before the simulator is hydraulically raised, and motion turned on. The cockpit is an exact replica of the GR.5, and the simulator can be instantly initialised to the location of your choice, with engine running, checks complete and fuel and water as required for the mission.

I had already listed all the manoeuvres that I wanted to include. A short take-off run employing the Harrier's greater than one-to-one power/weight ratio; a fast low pass and aerobatic manoeuvres to demonstrate the impressive turning performance; a rapid nozzled deceleration and a jet-borne sequence. My aim was to achieve balance, contrasting slow with fast manoeuvres, vertical with horizontal aerobatics, with equal weight on either side of crowd centre, and most importantly, attempting to keep the sequence as tight as possible, so as to avoid competition from the hamburger stands.

The 'full show' required three miles (4.8 km) visibility and no more than two octas cloud (2/8ths cloud cover) below 5000 ft (1524 m). In poorer conditions the programme degrades to a 'rolling show'. Although it should be possible to determine the type of display to be flown before strapping in, occasionally circumstances dictate a change of profile, perhaps even as late as mid-way through a sortie. For this reason, I attempted to design a rolling show as similar to the full programme as possible, substituting vertical with oblique manoeuvres, and a rolling vertical landing (RVL) bounce for the loop.

With its jet-borne capability, the Harrier's repertoire also includes a V/STOL (vertical, short

take-off and landing) show to be flown in conditions as poor as 0.62 mile (1km) visibility and 200 ft (60 m) cloud base. It was pointed out to me that on such occasions, since so few aircraft would be displaying, time is on my side. The display therefore includes a rest period to enable the engine limitations to be observed.

THE FIRST PRACTICE

The approval procedure took longer than anticipated, but on 11 February 1993, clearance to fly below 5000 ft (1500 m) was granted. By then, I had already flown the aerobatic manoeuvres at height, and was ready to piece together the choreographed sequence. Unfortunately, a 1200-ft (360 m) cloud base and 25-kt wind prevented the full show from being flown, but being extremely keen to get 'wheels in the well', I flew the second half of the sequence from the 100-ft (30 m) pass to the end, using Wittering's tower as display centre, with a visiting group of military dignitaries as my audience.

On the following Monday, northerly winds gusting up to 35 kts again restricted the performance, but it was possible to fly the looping manoeuvres using a base height of 1500 ft (450 m) and later 1000 ft (300 m) – a valuable exercise for calculating gate heights. On 16 February conditions were at last acceptable; two to three octas at 6000 ft (1800 m), reasonable visibility and a 20-kt wind. At 0745, the station commander, Gp Capt Day, briefed and authorised the flight, and then proceeded to the tower with Wg Cdr Harper (OC No 20[R] Sqn), Sqn Ldr Chambers (my immediate boss) plus a video team to record the event for debriefing purposes. The aircraft had been fuelled to 3000 lbs (1350 kg), just over a third of its normal load, and stood among the composite line of OCU jets.

I climbed into the roomy cockpit, signalled removal of the intake blanks, and fired up the auxiliary power unit, providing aircraft power for

ABOVE: Once the pilot has performed a detailed visual ground inspection of the jet, he will climb aboard and prime the avionic systems before engine start. A vital part of the pre-flight cockpit activity involves setting the aircraft's advanced ECM-resistant GEC Marconi Avionics AD3500 U/VHF-AM/FM communications equipment to the frequencies of the day, enabling the pilot to converse with both military and civil air traffic controllers. A display pilot transiting from one venue to the next during the course of a weekend needs to keep tabs on a variety of other aircraft, which requires a handful of frequencies, so a sophisticated comms fit like that in the GR.7 is a must

inertial platform alignment – a lengthy process than can be initiated before the external checks for expedience. Switching on the two multi-purpose colour displays (MPCDs), I inserted the aircraft datum position via the up-front controller, reading the seven-digit latitude and longitude from beside the aircraft on the pan. The MPCDs access most of the systems, removing the need for banks of switches, but also preventing a cursory glance from picking up any omissions.

Climbing out again, I completed the 'externals'. A plethora of questions from the ground-crew fuelled my mounting excitement. Strapping in, I adjusted the seat and rudder pedals, completed the 'left to rights', and after closing the bubble canopy, fired up the engine. Despite the painful whine outside the cockpit, the Pegasus engine could barely be heard from inside, my attention instead focusing on the vast array of lights and displays that had leapt into life. By pressing a selection of keys on the MPCDs, I initiated the numerous built-in tests (BITs) incorporated into most of the systems – engine BITs, fuel BITs, communications, navigation, IFF, rad alt and even control surface BITs. Gradually the warnings and cautions extinguished as the tests were successfully completed.

I waved the chocks away, and taxied forward of the line of silent aircraft, checking the brakes and nose-wheel steering connection. Even with its idling rpm at just 25 per cent, frequent dabs of the brakes, and, once clear of dispersal, down-

LEFT: Following a 6g max rate turn flown at full power, Rob rolls out and pitches hard to an attitude of 60° nose up for the climb into the half-Cuban positioning manoeuvre. He gains almost 4000 ft in a matter of seconds during this phase of his display

BELOW: Perfectly framed by the canopy's built-in mild detonating cord, which ensures that the perspex has shattered before the pilot passes through it should he have to eject, Rob puts his GR.7 through its paces at height during the display work-up phase

ABOVE: Captured in the middle of the inverted run, ZD466 reveals many details of its underside not usually exposed to the camera. Both inner pylons carry a weapons store, the one on the left an old Matra SNEB 155 rocket pod and on the right an empty CBLS No 200 practice bomb carrier. From this angle the size of the enlarged composite wing on the GR.5/7 can be fully appreciated

RIGHT: After the fast pass and 7g break, Rob decelerates for a mini-circuit and the first of the jet bounce manoeuvres. Illustrating the latter routine, ZD402 cruises along at about 100 kts, with its trailing edge 'positive circulation' wide-chord flaps fully extended and ailerons slightly drooped. The engine nozzles, which provide virtually all of the lift at low speed, have been rotated to a near vertical position, and the blow-in doors have also opened fully

ward rotation of the nozzles are required to prevent the aircraft from accelerating to an unacceptable speed. Up to 60° nozzle deflection is normally sufficient to reduce the rearward component of thrust.

Before lining-up, I stopped, running the nozzles aft to avoid burning the taxyway; set flaps to automatic, engine rating to combat, and con-firmed pins out and visuals to V/STOL, enabling JPT (Jet Pipe Temperature), rpm, nozzle and flap angles to be seen in the head-up display (HUD). With brakes applied, I set 55 per cent rpm (the maximum that the brakes will hold), nozzles to 20° and then, releasing the brakes, slammed on full power. My first display was under way.

The engine spools up to its 21,000 lbs

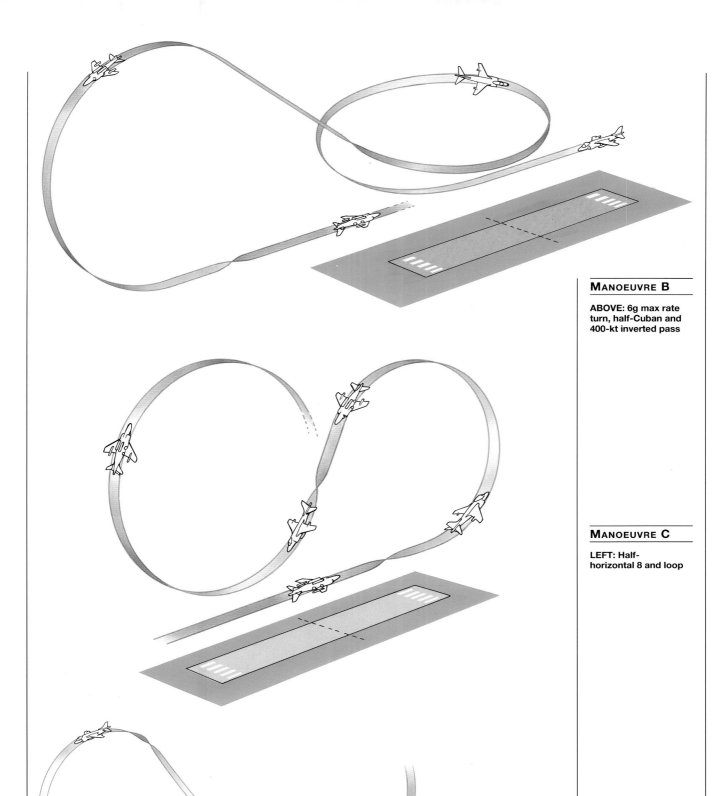

MANOEUVRE B

ABOVE: 6g max rate turn, half-Cuban and 400-kt inverted pass

MANOEUVRE C

LEFT: Half-horizontal 8 and loop

MANOEUVRE D

LEFT: 50° climb to wing-under, followed by 480-kt+ fast pass

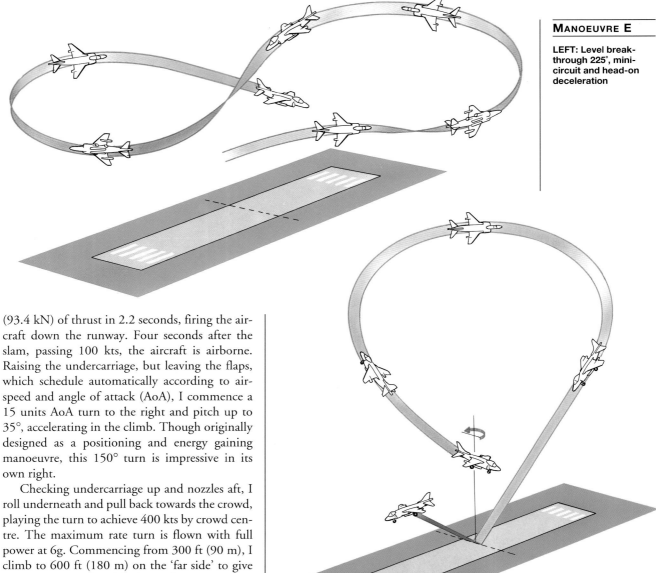

(93.4 kN) of thrust in 2.2 seconds, firing the air-craft down the runway. Four seconds after the slam, passing 100 kts, the aircraft is airborne. Raising the undercarriage, but leaving the flaps, which schedule automatically according to air-speed and angle of attack (AoA), I commence a 15 units AoA turn to the right and pitch up to 35°, accelerating in the climb. Though originally designed as a positioning and energy gaining manoeuvre, this 150° turn is impressive in its own right.

Checking undercarriage up and nozzles aft, I roll underneath and pull back towards the crowd, playing the turn to achieve 400 kts by crowd cen-tre. The maximum rate turn is flown with full power at 6g. Commencing from 300 ft (90 m), I climb to 600 ft (180 m) on the 'far side' to give the impression of level flight. Rolling out, I pitch hard to 60° nose up for the half-Cuban, climbing to the gate of 4500 ft (1350 m) at 200 kts. This is the first of several positioning manoeuvres, selected both for upwind penetration and to enable the base height to be regained away from crowd centre for the inverted run.

Fuel and oil considerations limit the inverted pass to 15 seconds, after which a half-horizontal 8 re-positions the aircraft for a tight loop. Enter-ing from 350 kts, the Harrier loops inside 4000 ft (1200 m), a figure comparable with agile jets like the Hawk, maintaining good control authority throughout. Turning away and pitching up 50°, I fly a wing-under allowing the aircraft to acceler-ate. Achieving 450 kts for the 100 ft (30 m) pass is not a problem.

Beginning the transition from wing-borne to jet-borne flight, I break away with a 7g pull, selecting idle thrust and airbrakes out. A quick check of fuel ensures hover performance, then decelerating though 300 kts I move the nozzle

control (located next to the throttle) fully aft, running nozzles to the braking position and simultaneously powering the reaction controls, situated at the aircraft's extremes. Pushing the control column well forward to counteract the large trim forces, the left hand moves back to the throttle to select full power. During the rapid deceleration from 300 to 80 kts, control of height gradually changes from the elevators, via the con-trol column, to the throttle. From herein, the laws of aerodynamics and flight become con-fused, as the complications resulting from vec-tored thrust come into play. Aircraft attitude and nozzle angle now control flight path.

Aiming to achieve 80 kts abeam crowd centre, nozzles are selected to 73° (8° forward of the vertical setting) to maintain speed – each 1° of nozzle equates to 10 kts of forward speed –

LEFT: Following several aerobatic sorties flown at medium level in late January 1993, Rob was finally given permission to practice his full routine at 'airshow' heights the following month. Although adverse weather initially played havoc with his work-ups, by the time Rob performed his full display in front of the AOC at Wittering on 21 April, the 10-minute routine had been flown on numerous occasions and had become almost second nature to him. Lining up ZD466 for a 450-kt pass over crowd centre at the minimum hard deck height of 100 ft, the pilot gently banks over the farmland that surrounds Wittering

and I commence mini-circuit to the right.

This is a tricky manoeuvre to fly as the aircraft is directionally unstable at low speeds. If sideslip is allowed to develop, uncontrolled roll can result with little or no warning. For this reason, the aircraft has several vital sideslip indicators, including a simple, but very effective, weather-type vane, a slip ball in the HUD, and rudder-pedal shakers.

Pointing at crowd centre, I select undercarriage down, flaps to 62° and decelerate to the hover. Once stationary, nozzles and power are quickly adjusted and then depressing the rudder control, the aircraft spot turns through 180° using the reaction controls.

The climbing acceleration is an exercise in co-ordination. 'Normal' accelerations from the hover are flown with a level flight path by selecting an excess of power, then with the left hand firmly on the nozzle lever, gradually moving the nozzles aft to maintain level flight. As the aircraft accelerates and gains aerodynamic lift, less vertical thrust is required, enabling further nozzle movement. If nozzle movement is too slow, the aircraft climbs and vice versa. In the climbing acceleration, however, pitching the aircraft complicates matters by changing the true angle of the column of thrust, and so the exercise becomes one of fine judgement if the aircraft is to continue accelerating whilst pitching up.

Passing 1000 ft (300 m), I roll right and pull back towards the crowd. The aircraft returns to conventional flight as the nozzles have been moved aft, but they are once again required, together with power, to decelerate and maintain 80 kts as the jet descends to RVL (Rolling Vertical Landing) bounce abeam

crowd centre. This is flown with a fixed nozzle angle (close to the hover position), using variations in power.

After the bounce, the nimble left hand moves quickly to the nozzle lever, selecting the braking position, back to the throttle to arrest the climb, and back to the nozzles again selecting 81° of nozzle when the aircraft has decelerated to a standstill.

Turning 90° towards the crowd and then, by simply tilting the aircraft and therefore the thrust vector, the jet is flown sideways to datum. This manoeuvre is more effective when flown downwind due to its aerodynamic limit of 30 kts airspeed.

The now infamous bow is flown by simultaneously moving the control column forward, at the same time as progressively rotating the noz-

MANOEUVRE G

BELOW: 90° sideways to datum, bow, 270° spot turn, back-up and RVL

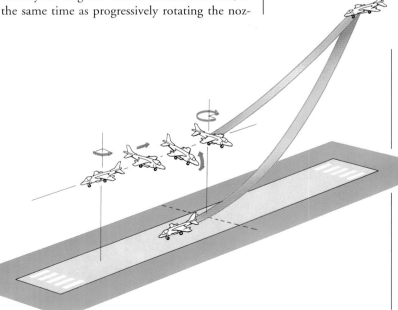

zles to the braking position so as to maintain a vertical column of thrust. Out of the bow, I turn through 270° and fly backwards, climbing to a position that enables a landing to be made at crowd centre from an RVL.

In the nine minutes it's taken you to read this chapter I've flown my display, but feel as though I've been through a full hour's sortie. Concentration and exertion give way to relief as I taxy back for a frank debrief with the station commander, and a review of the video.

With one display complete, the routine of my work-up had begun. Arriving at the squadron at 0715, I would select the display to be flown, having first spoken to the duty meteorological forecaster, and calculated manoeuvre headings based upon his surface and 3000-ft winds. A couple of minutes with the squadron's 'V/STOL' computer enabled the aircraft's take-

BELOW: The most popular phase of the Harrier's airshow routine is the complex V/STOL segment flown towards the end of the display. This part of the display is also the most demanding for aircraft and pilot alike, both relying solely on the Harrier's 'big hearted' Rolls-Royce Pegasus turbofan engine to provide sufficient thrust to stay aloft. Slick manipulation of the nozzle control lever in conjunction with the airbrakes, and control column, enable Rob to decelerate rapidly from 300 to 80 kts. Being careful not to allow sideslip to develop, the pilot slows to the hover, lowering the gear as he passes through 80 kts

off and hover performance to be determined, and then having filled in the authorisation sheets, I would telephone the station commander to discuss my intentions and highlight perceived problems.

No two displays were the same; sometimes a low cloud base would be the focus of my attention, whilst the next day cloud problems would be replaced by a 20-kt on-crowd wind. On another occasion, the wind might be off-crowd, making the previously applied corrections, designed to cater for the wind, inappropriate. For all display pilots, wind constitutes a major factor requiring careful consideration prior to the performance, particulalry if the display is to remain anchored at crowd centre. When in conventional wingborne flight, the Harrier suffers wind-induced position keeping problems in the same way as other fast jets, but it is whilst in the jet-borne regime that it is most at risk from the effects of wind.

As an example, when hovering in a 20-kt head-wind, although stationary with respect to the ground, the aircraft is actually flying forwards through the 'air' at 20 kts, this being

achieved by either moving the nozzles aft 2°, or lowering the nose by the same amount. If the aircraft is now turned through 90°, so that the wind is all across, although still in the hover, the aircraft is now effectively flying sideways at 20 kts, having lost its forward speed. In the turn, therefore, the nose down attitude must gradually be replaced by into-wind bank if the aircraft is to remain stationary. Power requirements are also affected during this turn; reaction controls, applied to initiate the turn, bleed thrust from the aircraft's vertical column, and wing lift reduces as the air that flowed over the wings changes to a cross-wind.

Although hovering in windy conditions is not as straight forward as it might appear, it is a skill that is well practised by all Harrier pilots. A part of my display that is not so routinely flown, however, is the sideways and backwards translations. These manoeuvres have a 30-kt airspeed limit which, if exceeded, would result in a loss of control. For this reason, real care and precision are required. Unfortunately, there is no air speed indication whilst flying sideways or backwards. However, an exact round speed readout in the cockpit, together with the wind speed and direction announced by air traffic, enables me to calculate the limiting ground speed for the day. To increase the effectiveness of the manoeuvres, they are flown downwind whenever possible.

The 'bow' or 'nod' is another manoeuvre significantly affected by

the wind. Although flown on the odd occasion by all Harrier pilots (you never know when you might be required to impress), the bow is normally only attempted whilst pointing into wind. Of course, as a display pilot, I have no control over either the location of the crowd or, the direction of the wind, and

must therefore be able to bow whilst pointing at the crowd, whatever the wind direction.

As mentioned earlier, backwards translations cannot be flown above 30 kts airspeed, and with a 30-kt on-crowd wind, whilst pointing at the crowd in the hover, I am effectively flying backwards at that speed! 'Bowing' in these conditions must be performed carefully to avoid an uncontrollable pitching down of the nose caused by the

RIGHT: Hovering for several seconds, Rob uses rudder control inputs to manipulate the reaction control valves (RCVs), swinging the Harrier through 180°. He then commences a climbing acceleration away from the crowd, and passing through 1000 ft, rolls to the right and pulls the aircraft back towards the crowd. The nozzles are used once again to wash off excess speed as the pilot repositions for a rolling vertical landing (RVL) abeam crowd centre. As can be seen in this photograph, the bounce is flown with the nozzles fixed at an angle close to the hover position. Rob practised RVLs on both tarmac and grass at Wittering, using similar approach performance parameters for both surfaces

wind 'lifting' the tail. To make matters worse, when travelling backwards, or hovering with a tailwind, although the reaction controls function normally, the elevators tend to work in the opposite sense.

As my work-up continued, my understanding and experience of 'extreme V/STOL' grew. I found that, with practice, slightly less of my capacity was required to fly the aircraft, thus leaving me with more time to think and plan ahead.

From the beginning of my work-up, I treated Wittering's airfield as a display site, with its own simulated crowd line and display centre. Very strict rules govern how close aircraft can approach the crowd, the distance depending upon speed and velocity vector; ie, whether the aircraft is pointing towards the crowd or not. For straight flypasts, parallel to the crowd, the aircraft can fly as close as 230 m. In a turn, during which there is an on-crowd vector, the minimum distance increases to 450 m. For jet-borne manoeuvres, I can close to 110 m.

To enable me to gain practice flying to the 'lines', I studied a 50,000 scale map of the airfield to find ground features that were exactly 110, 230 and 450 m away from my simulated crowd front. This would enable me to visualise the lines from the air, in an attempt to fly as close as possible without infringing the rules. At a show, flying outside the minimum distances, although safe, would reduce the effectiveness of the performance, but flying too close and infringing the rules could result in a premature end to the show, following an order to land.

By the middle of March, the date for the AOC's check had been set. I had four weeks to complete my preparations, but it was not just a matter of sorting out the flying. On the ground, there was an ever in-creasing pile of letters to be answered. The list of shows for the 93 season had been finalised and immediately following its publication, the first of many questionnaires from eager display organisers had arrived.

The task of deciding which aircraft will display where is centrally controlled by the Air Force Displays' Office, and the Participation Committee. Towards the end of each year, units that are providing display pilots state the number of displays that they are able to support, based upon perceived operational commitments, manning and aircraft availability for the following year. The participation committee then meet and attempt to match the RAF's assets with the requests from display organisers. Unfortunately, participation requests massively exceed resources, but each case is examined on its own merit, and the RAF's aircraft are carefully divided amongst the shows, giving the highest priority to Battle of Britain and RAF at home days, and then considering major civilian shows and other open days. Lists of the events at which each aircraft will participate are published in the spring, after which the administrative process gets under way.

Everything from fuel and oil details to parking and accommodation needed solving. To help prepare for the displays, aerial photographs, 50,000-scale maps and airfield approach details for each of the sites were applied for.

Fortunately, much help was at hand. Sqn Ldr Mike Young, the nominated display manager, sorted out our finances, support and publication of PR material. Chief Tech Gerry Langstaff, with

three years display experience behind him, organised the engineering support carefully picking each team, and relaying our many requirements to the show organisers. Also, Flt Lt Rob Blake, a student pilot holding between basic and advanced flying training, manned the telephone on a daily basis, trouble shooting for the team, whilst we were otherwise engaged on primary duties.

After a thorough work-up period, one hurdle remained – the AOC's check. Every year the AOC of No 1 Group visits a nominated airfield to review the proposed displays of his command's aircraft. For the display crews, this is the final judgement, but it is by no means a 'rubber stamp'. If the AOC is not happy with the performance, it will fail, preventing the crew from performing in front of the public.

This year the Harrier was hosting the event, and so on 21 April a small airshow took place over the skies of Wittering as the Jaguar, Tornado GR.1 and Harrier crews each flew their sequences in front of the AOC. Fortunately, we all received his seal of approval. In three weeks' time we would be flying our first real display. □

BELOW: Four nozzles of vectored thrust operate like a quartet of 'super' vacuum cleaners in reverse, kicking up a plume or debris when operating off of an unpaved strip. The pilot has to be precise with his landing speed to avoid sucking debris into the intake. 55 kts is the approved touchdown speed, providing the Harrier with enough forward momentum to keep the intakes ahead of the mini 'dust storm' following in the jet's wake – a few knots less and the squadron engineers will have to strip the Pegasus down and clean out the grass (Photo by John Dibbs)

THE SEASON

MY FIRST show was at North Weald on 15/16 May 1993. Despite thorough preparation I was quite nervous as the big day approached. On Friday, after my arrival, I had booked a ten-minute slot for practice. There was just enough time to dash up to the tower to discuss my routine with the display director before putting it into practice.

There are quite a lot of factors that need careful consideration before leaping into the air for a practice or a display. Some of the required information could be gleaned from the information pack sent out by the display organisers some weeks beforehand such as the display axis; location of the 230 and 450 m lines, and how they will be marked; position of the crowds, crowd centre and the public car parks (which must not be overflown); local obstacles; radio frequencies; holding, joining, R/T failure and crash procedures; aircraft taxying and parking areas; and briefing and display times. However, a number of details critical for the Harrier were not provided and had to be examined on arrival.

As my routine includes two periods of hovering, it is helpful to consider the exact layout of the proposed crowd line in order to decide whether to hover in the same place twice, or in the case of a long drawn-out crowd, to hover once at either end. Also, one of the approaches to the hover is flown at right angles to the crowd line, and there-

RIGHT: In the circuit, seconds away from the break to land, Rob photographed Flt Lt Woore against the colourful backdrop of the RAF Finningley car and caravan park upon their arrival at the South Yorkshire base for the 1993 Battle of Britain 'At Home' Air Day. This event was one of the largest at which the Harrier Team performed all season, and was the second display flown on 18 September, the first-taking place at RAF Leuchars, in Scotland, as part of their Air Day celebrations

ABOVE: There is no mistaking the White Cliffs of Dover as the backdrop for this 'close up' portrait of Sqn Ldr Mike Young. Usually, military jets transit from one airfield to the next at high level so as to avoid the civil light aircraft traffic which tends to clutter the skies at the weekends. However, complications associated with controlled airspace, particularly over areas surrounding London and the South East, prevented a high-level transit on this occasion, and the Harrier pilots were forced to keep a diligent lookout for microlights and gliders as they skirted London on their way back to Wittering from France

TOP RIGHT: Rob follows his leader over the Irish Sea, heading for RAF Aldergrove and the Ulster Airshow. Once in Northern Ireland, the Harrier Display Team performed in front of a huge, if slightly wet, crowd in Newtownards. This performance was in jeopardy right up to the last moment as a large terrorist bomb had devastated the town centre in the week preceding Rob's display. The letter symbology at the bottom of the HUD screen shows: R - RPM at 80 per cent; J - jet pipe temperature at 416°F; 0 - 0° nozzle angle (horizontal); and F - flap angle at 5°, which is the standard cruise setting. The figure '406' represents the jet's speed in knots

ABOVE: During the transit from Wittering to Aldergrove on 10 July 1993, Rob's route took him over his old student stamping ground of Port Erin on the Isle of Man. In this wonderfully 'atmospheric' view of ZD347, taken as the jets overflew the southern tip of the Island, a faint cloud of moisture can be seen forming over the aircraft's centre wing section, emphasizing just how damp those menacing clouds in the background really were!

fore involves jet-borne flight away from the runway. Before performing this manoeuvre, it is prudent to first investigate the security of the display markers to avoid re-arranging the layout. On this occasion, I was advised of the location of a number of explosives placed on the ground beside the runway to be detonated during a simulated air-

field attack part-way into the show. Obviously, I would have to avoid those areas, and this also negated a bounce on the grass.

I taxied out for my practice on time, having first checked that the day was running to plan. A few late arrivals begged permission to land from air traffic. This was granted and I watched my

ABOVE: More islands, but this time on a much finer day. Flt Lt Woore is seen cruising off the coast of Guernsey on 16 September 1993 prior to recovering at the small airport well in time for the afternoon show. The huge transparency covering the aircraft's cockpit allows you to clearly see into the pilot's spacious 'office'

greeted us at the display briefing. The Tucano's engine had been contaminated with shale, and would require an engine change. Our aircraft had also been tampered with, an intake cover having been removed. Realising the potentially disastrous consequences that would follow a power-plant failure during a display, the engineers elected to carry out a precautionary engine run on both the primary display jet and the second Harrier that we had brought along as a spare.

One of the aircraft refused to start, the cause later being traced to an incorrectly positioned engineer's switch located behind the ejection seat which must have also been tampered with overnight. This act of vandalism left us all feeling rather uncomfortable, but I'm pleased to say that it was the only incident of its type that we experienced during the season.

Both shows at North Weald went smoothly, increasing my confidence and proving the value of the weeks of training. On the Saturday, in addition to the North Weald show, I displayed at Ipswich International Airport. A rather unusual venue, Ipswich has no hardened runways, just two short grass strips, thus making it somewhat less 'International' than its name implies. For this reason I elected to conduct a pre-display recce in the week preceding the show.

Although the Harrier is capable of operating away from conventional tarmac or concrete runways, the surface needs to be be firm enough to support the aircraft's 18,000-lb mass. If the ground is too soft, the aircraft will sink, or 'bog-in', as this phenomena is called. To avoid such an alarming predicament occuring, the condition of the operating surface must first be measured with the aid of a penetrometer, or 'pogo stick/prodder' as it is known in the trade.

Following a two-hour drive to Ipswich, Chief Tech Langstaff and I, with airfield map and 'pogo stick' in hand (but no form of communication with the circling aircraft), began a survey of the runways. Taking measurements from an active strip proved quite amusing, but within an hour we had marked all the unsuitable ground, and planned my exact taxy, take-off and landing areas. Returning to Wittering, I listened attentively to the weather forecasts in the days leading up to the show. Heavy rain would prevent a landing, but as luck would have it, a dry spell enabled me to fly the first military jet into Ipswich International.

On Monday morning with three displays complete, I flew to Marham to preposition for an afternoon display as part of No 617 Sqn's 50th Anniversary celebrations. A 25-kt on-crowd wind added a little spice to the hovering, but otherwise the display proceeded rather uneventfully, bring-

fuel steadily burn down as I held to the west of the runway. Then to my surprise a number of 'warbirds' carried out a second unscheduled practice.

Few aircraft display with full fuel tanks because of the associated penalty and reduced performance. In the Harrier's case, it is imperative that I carry as little fuel as possible to enable prolonged hovering without causing unreasonable engine wear. I knew exactly how much fuel was consumed during my show, and elected to carry an extra 'two-minutes' worth as a precaution. With such safety margins, it does not take much holding on the ground to remove the flex, and on this sortie (my first practice) I could only fly half of the show before being forced to land on my fuel reserves. I was learning fast.

The following morning, unpalatable news

ABOVE: Whilst not exactly bucket and spade weather, the popularity of the Harrier ensured that it was virtually standing room only in Sunderland when the jet performed over a grey and choppy North Sea in August 1993 *(Photo by Suzanne Lea)*

ing my first full weekend to a successful close.

Two weeks later, after a pleasant weekend displaying in France, I performed at Mildenhall and

Southend. Strong winds prevailed for the entire weekend. At Mildenhall it was unfortunate that the wind direction was perpendicular to the runway, as this resulted in the withdrawal of a large number of participants, with the cross-wind exceeding their limit.

Although the Harrier is capable of taking-off and landing in very high winds, I would normally close my show with a vertical landing, which has a 15-kt crosswind limit. It was obvious therefore, that if I were to display I would need to overshoot from my 'RVL bounces' and vertically land at the end. Contrary to popular belief, the Harrier cannot land vertically anywhere. Attempting this manoeuvre over unprotected grass would create a hole as big as a bomb crater, and soil ingestion would surge the engine. Over tarmac, the 750° C air would melt the surface, and pebbledash the underside of the aircraft. The only suitable surface is concrete. Fortunately, Mildenhall, like many large bases, boasts a runway with concrete thresholds, which admirably suited my purpose, and thus enabled the Harrier to display.

After my second performance at Mildenhall, I flew down to Southend. This would be my first seaside venue. With a clearly defined crowd-line (the beach) and no chimneys or sensitive areas to avoid, a seaside display should be relatively straight forward. However, experiences have proven otherwise. Calm weather promotes the most dangerous conditions. A mirror-like sea surface can distort the assessment of height, making recoveries from the vertical hazardous and requiring total reliance on the altimeter. A poorly defined horizon, which often accompanies sum-

ABOVE LEFT: Not the place to perform an RVL! Rob shows off the GR.7's hovering ability within the confines of Guernsey Harbour. Throughout the display, Rob kept a good lookout for stray aircraft (or seagulls). Although untroubled by fellow aviators (either in man-made craft or of the feathered variety) during his performance, Rob was forced to keep a wary eye on a spectator in a speedboat, who was hell bent on stripping off the paintwork on his vessel by trying to position himself underneath the GR.7's jet wash *(Photo by Suzanne Lea)*

ABOVE RIGHT: Spreading the good word about the RAF, and in particular the Harrier, is just as important a task for the Display Team as flying the jet to entertain the assembled crowd. Mike Young is an expert at PR, and no doubt inspired dozens of would-be aviators to rush off to their local recruiting offices and sign up to be GR.5/7 pilots. Despite the 'armchair aviating' going on in the cockpit above, No 20(R) Sqn engineer Cpl Stokes presses on with his turn-round checks on the nose gear leg

RIGHT: Of all the tasks performed by the groundcrew on the aircraft both before and after a display, easily the most onerous is the refilling of its de-mineralised water tank. In this photograph taken at Manston on 5 September 1993, the short straw has been drawn by Junior Tech Allsop, who is having to hand-pump the contents of the blue drum into the Harrier's 50 gal water tank. The water is used to cool the hot exhaust gases during the display, thus enabling the engine to run at a higher RPM and therefore deliver more thrust – an extra 1000 lbs+ to be precise. It also serves to reduce engine fatigue because the power-plant can run at a cooler temperature

RIGHT: Looking a little perplexed by the Form 700s in the file on his lap, Flt Lt Spike Newbery fills in the paperwork and has the 'brews' ready for Rob's return following his display at RAF Valley. Spike was a model 'number two', or ferry pilot, throughout the season, dealing with the forms and getting the jets rapidly turned around whilst Rob was mentally preparing himself for the next performance

ABOVE: Ray-Bans to the fore, Chief Tech Gerry Langstaff, the team's chief engineer, and display manager Sqn Ldr Mike Young confer over the flying programme at the Sunderland Airshow. Gerry wears the once familiar Welsh wild cat patch of No 233 OCU above his right breast pocket

mer afternoons, can induce disorientation and loss of situational awareness. Yachtsmen and boat owners keen to improve their view have been known to venture into the display arena, bringing with them their own obstacles in the form of tall masts. Coast lines are also notorious for concentrations of birds, which constitute a major hazard when travelling at over 500 kts.

As I held in an orbit 15 miles to the east of Southend, waiting for the preceding act to finish, it was obvious that I would not have to worry about hazy conditions or mirror-like seas. The visibility was excellent and a 25-kt southerly wind whipped up the sea and kept most of the gulls on the ground. With a few minutes to go, I checked my fuel quantity and balance, while setting up the 'bingo warning'. This simple, but effective, device sounds alarm bells in my headset when the fuel in the aircraft's tanks reaches a previously calculated level that I've set on the gauge. When it rings it means that it's time to land, or in this case, that I've got just enough fuel to transit from the display site to the nearest airfield and land.

I rolled inverted to check harness security and to ensure that there were no loose articles in the cockpit, then flew a 'max rate' turn to warm up for the coming performance. A speeded up mental rehearsal of my routine served to refresh the sequence in my mind, thinking through the order of roll directions, speed and height gates, as well as crowd positioning. I carried a copy of all four display sequences, together with wind corrected headings, on my kneepad, following the advice of a now retired, but experienced, display pilot. He had told me that however well you think you know your sequence, it is possible in the heat of battle to lose your place, have a mental block or be unable to recall the next manoeuvre.

Just to re-emphasise this warning, I was told the tale of another pilot who inadvertently flew the wrong manoeuvre, thereby missing out a whole chunk of his display – a similar mistake would have serious implications in the Harrier as you tried to hover with more than the planned fuel weight. By the end of the season, I could not recall even one occasion when I had looked at my kneepad during the display, but it had proved reassuring, and therefore served its purpose.

Holding at Southend with one minute to go, the previous act called complete. I turned onto a westerly heading, descended to 300 ft, and accelerated to 420 kts, calling 'Wildcat, running-in'. It was now that I realised the value of the time that I had previously spent studying the approach. There was the bend in the coast, the small inlet and the pier, with the 230 and 450 m lines being marked by dayglo panels hanging from its sides. I lined up over the nearest marker and began my

ABOVE: The ear-splitting whine of a Pegasus idling has caused many babies to cry, dogs to bark, wives to wince and car alarms to go off over the past 30 years or so, and here the crowd at Cranfield Airshow are exposed to the throaty roar of a Rolls-Royce engine at close quarters. Following the HUD symbology clockwise from the nine o'clock position, the '-6.0' figure is angle of attack, the instrument not functioning correctly whilst the aircraft is stationary on the ramp; the number '30' is the indicated airspeed, which does not read values below 30 kts; the horizontal line of numbers reflects the aircraft's heading (342° true when this photograph was taken); '200' is the altimeter reading in feet, this number being reset to zero by the pilot immediately prior to launch; '0.0 WYPT 2' stands for Waypoint 2, which is the waypoint designated in the GR.7's inertial navigation system (INS) by Rob to indicate the position of Cranfield, the '0.0' reading denoting that he has not moved from his dialled in position; and finally '14:52:23' is Greenwich meantime!

RIGHT: Even with Spike's help, the Form 700s still require the display pilot's perusal and signature following his walk-round check of the jet. Satisfied that his GR.5 is up to the task at hand, Rob signs the Harrier out prior to his performance in front of a full house at Cambrai air base in France on 22 May 1993. The small rectangular cut out in the wing tip immediately in front of the formation light is the port reaction control valve, one of five such devices fitted to the Harrier which allow the pilot to manoeuvre the jet both horizontally and vertically whilst in the hover
(Photo by Suzanne Lea)

search for the centre of the crowd – travelling at 700 ft per second, I didn't have a whole lot of time in which to acquire it. Seeing my reference point, I performed one last check of my speed and height, and then abeam crowd centre, I snapped into the max-rate turn. The show was underway

On 5 June, I was amused by an incident that followed a display in Scotland. The venue was Faslane, and again I was performing over the sea, this time with my display centred on a short pier beside Faslane's large naval base. As Glasgow Airport was only about 15 miles away, I had planned to recover there on completion of my routine. Hearing of my plans, the organiser asked if, on departure, I could route via a ship pre-positioned in front of crowd centre as part of a set piece drama that would see the vessel disabled shortly after I had passed over it by a number of controlled explosions from simulated bombs. A rigid raider, crawling with Marines, would then carry out a daring rescue of a distressed maiden held captive on the bow, recovering the damsel triumphantly to the pier. When I asked how I would recognise this vessel, he replied, 'It'll be the only one in the display area.' Nothing could be simpler.

To this day, I'm still not sure how such a straight forward plan could go so badly wrong, but on reaching the venue, I was horrified to find the area teeming with boats. Large ones, small ones, yachts, inflatables, and I'm sure somewhere hidden amongst them all, a distressed maiden. As I flew south at the end of my show, I attempted to line up as many of the boats as possible, in the vain hope that I could save the day. Having flown past the line I looked over my shoulder for any sign of success. Seeing no explosions, I transferred my gaze further afield, but to no avail. No smoke, no Marines and I can only assume, one smitten maiden.

Engineering support for aircraft attending airshows is a controversial topic amongst display pilots and organisers. Obviously the organiser would like each aircraft to display for the minimum cost. However, what constitutes the minimum level of engineering support to guarantee a show varies from one aircraft type to another. The Harrier is quite unusual in this respect. Despite a high serviceability rate, aircraft turnarounds require more expertise, manpower and time than the 'pilot-supervised topping up of fuel' that characterises a number of other types. For a start, accurate refuelling is critical in order to prevent lateral imbalance which would cause embarrassment whilst hovering. Fifty gallons of demineralised water needs to be transported to the venue and painstakingly hand-pumped onboard via a port on the spine of the jet. Regular inspections of

RIGHT: Rob flew over 50 displays at events across Great Britain and Western Europe, and although the summer of 1993 won't be remembered as a vintage season for sun, the Harrier Display Team only suffered one wash out – Pornichet Airshow, which was to be staged over the beaches of St Nazaire on 13/14 July. However, the weather conditions seen in this dramatic photograph testify to the fact that the routine flown at the St Mawgan Open Day three weeks later was right on the limits. Captured on film performing the RVL bounce, Rob was asked to fly not once, but twice in Cornwall because most of the other jets on the programme were grounded due to the weather. The Harrier's low cloud limit is 200 ft for its V/STOL display, so the cloud base has to be essentially on the runway to force the jet to sit out an entire show (Photo by John Durston)

LEFT: Cruising over the neatly kept farmland of eastern Suffolk, Rob's wingman dumps excess Avtur at high altitude during the transit to RAF Marham's Open Day on 17 May 1993. Fuel management of a gas-guzzling Pegasus II Mk 105 turbofan is a fine art learned with experience, the engine devouring 200 lbs of Avtur per minute during a standard display. Too much fuel in the tanks will result in unduly high engine counts due to the jet's hefty weight, whilst too little will cause an embarrassingly abrupt curtailment to the day's performance

ABOVE RIGHT: It's the small touches which are remembered by a seasoned display pilot following a hectic five months 'on the road'. Okay, so the beer may be Belgian, but at least it's cold and poured in the glass before the engine compressor fan blades have stopped ticking away behind you. The 'bar steward' was photographed on the ramp at Florennes Air Force Base on 28 August 1993

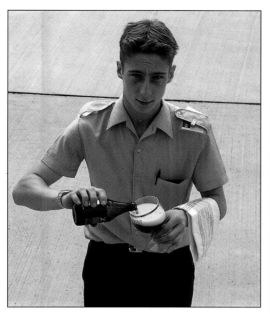

HARRIER DISPLAY TEAM'S 1993 DIARY

15 May	Fighter Meet, North Weald
15 May	Ipswich Air Fair
16 May	Fighter Meet, North Weald
17 May	No 617 Sqn 50th Anniversary, Marham
21 May	Upavon
22 May	FAF Cambrai (France)
29 May	RAF Mildenhall Fete 93
30 May	RAF Mildenhall Fete 93
30 May	Southend Airshow
31 May	Southend Airshow
5 June	Faslane Airshow
5 June	BAe Lostock Gala
12 June	RAF Coningsby Open Day
18 June	RAF Turnhouse
19 June	RAF Halton Open Day/Clophill Fete flypast
19 June	Biggin Hill Air Fair
20 June	Biggin Hill Air Fair
20 June	RAF Cosford Open Day
26 June	RAF St Athan Open Day
26 June	Woodford RAFA Airshow
27 June	RAF Swanton Morley Open Day
27 June	Mil Rally, Nostell Priory
2 July	RAF Waddington (RCDs)
3 July	RAF Waddington Open Day
10 July	Ulster Airshow
10 July	Wirral Airshow
13/14 July	Pornichet Airshow (France)
18 Jul	RAF Church Fenton SSAFA Air Day
18 July	Leicester/Bruntingthorpe Airshow
24/25 July	RAF Fairford/IAT
28 July	RAF Chivenor Open Day
31 July	RAF Leeming Open Day
4 Aug	RAF St Mawgan Open Day (two displays)
8 Aug	Jurby Air Show, Isle of Man
28/29 Aug	BAF Florennes (Belgium)
4 Sep	Shoreham
5 Sep	Manston
5 Sep	Shuttleworth/Old Warden
11 Sep	Benson
12 Sep	Southport
16 Sep	Guernsey
16 Sep	Jersey
18 Sep	RAF Finningley, BofB 'At Home' day
18 Sep	RAF Leuchars, BofB 'At Home' day
19 Sep	Cranfield Airshow
19 Sep	RAF Newton, BofB Families Day
20 Sep	BAF Bierset (Belgium)

the unprotected first stage compressor blades must be performed, engineers searching for nicks and cuts which can be caused by the ingestion of foreign objects from poorly swept runways. In the event of any damage being found, careful blending of the individual blades is required. Finally, ground handling of the aircraft, particularly on poorly prepared surfaces or grass strips, requires the help of a marshaller familiar with Harrier characteristics.

Despite occasional protests from event organisers, the majority of displays were supported by a small engineering team who zig-zagged across the country by road to the various sites. The team comprised one specialist from each of the five trade groups, namely engines, avionics, airframes, armourers and electricians, all supervised by a senior non-commissioned officer who could be from any one of these areas. As financial restraints prohibited RAF Wittering from opening over the weekend, I would have to transit to my first venue on a Friday afternoon, returning early on the Monday. The engineers, however, would have to deploy some considerable time before me, in order to prepare the ground for my arrival.

Engineering support was not only provided by the road party. Back at Wittering, before the deployment had commenced, two nominated display aircraft (plus a spare if available) needed preparing for the weekend, a routine which usually entailed declassifying the electronic warfare suite; checking the short forecast notes; bringing forward servicings that would otherwise expire during the weekend; topping up the oil to ferry; and of course ensuring the paperwork was in order. Whilst the aircraft were being prepared, the road party would be loading the 'four-tonner', and/or mini van, with everything from hydraulic

fluids to demineralised water. Also packed in for the weekend away was a complete set of spare tyres; a towing arm; intro-scope kit; water-pumps; a penetrometer, plus a host of other tools to enable them to cover as many foreseeable problems as vehicle space would allow. The size of the supporting task cannot be over-emphasised, but the system worked extremely well, a measure of our success being 57 out of 58 displays flown as scheduled.

The only venue at which the Harrier did not display was at Pornichet, in France, on 13/14 July. This event was to be staged over the sea in a large bay overlooked by miles of beach. The organisers were expecting a crowd of over a quarter of a million to descend on the town and watch the evening's spectacular aerial exhibition, played out against the backdrop of a setting sun.

Displaying overseas always complicates things – flight plans, route forecasts, and airfield approach aids are all necessary, and are usually only available in a foreign language! Prior to the

ABOVE: The husband and wife team of Rob and Suzanne Lea have travelled the length and breadth of the UK over the past 18 months. Suzanne actually outranks her husband during the week, serving just down the road from Wittering at RAF Brampton as a squadron leader in the Supply Branch

display, I had received little information from the organisers, but with the help of an RAF pilot on exchange with the French, we had managed to sort out the essentials. The ferry pilot was to be my boss, Wg Cdr Harper, whose interpreter-level French would prove extremely useful.

Our destination was St Nazaire, a military airfield 16 miles from the display site. We were amongst a handful of aircraft operating from St Nazaire, the other participants working from a small, but lively, airport situated just three miles from the beach. The Harrier could have quite happily operated from the airport's 3000-ft strip, but the French security services would not allow it.

Arriving at St Nazaire, I was surprised to hear that I was expected to fly a practice display that evening at 9 pm. As I had been instructing from 7.30 am that morning, I was less than keen on this idea, and so the organisers kindly agreed to bring my practice time forward. Before the practice I attended a simple display brief, at which the main point emphasised seemed to be that we were not to display over the northern end of the beach near Le Koul, but rather stay to the south in front of Pornichet, as they were paying for the show – a reasonable request, I thought. The practice went as planned, and on the following day I enjoyed a leisurely morning wind surfing from the beach as the Toyota aerobatic team embarked upon a catamaran race. The weather did not look promising, but there was still time for an improvement.

However, by the evening low cloud and drizzle covered the whole region, and a police helicopter was asked to carry out a weather check, after which the organisers were forced to cancel the show. Feeling rather frustrated, we were encouraged to visit the VIP tent, positioned on the beach at crowd centre, to socialise with the

dignitaries over a cocktail or two. The evening felt flat as we stood in the dripping tent, describing the displays that we had hoped to provide – the crowds would have to wait for next year.

Another display that almost didn't materialise was that at Newtownards, in Northern Ireland, scheduled for 10 July. I had visited here before, and so was quite looking forward to the event until, in the week preceding the show, the centre of Newtownards was devastated by an enormous bomb. Immediately, I realised that the weekend was in jeopardy, but was still prepared to display if the show was going ahead. Even as late as Friday morning the go/no decision had not been made. Eventually, with only a few hours remaining to our planned departure, we were given clearance to display, but were told that we would have to operate from RAF Aldergrove, 20 miles to the west of Newtownards.

Crossing the shores of Northern Ireland, I was astonished by the beauty of the country. As we transited west along the border, the majestic mountains of southern Ireland could be clearly seen. It was hard to believe the troubles that occurred amongst the green pastures. On the day, my display at Newtownards was perfectly timed to coincide with a heavy rainshower. However, this did not appear to affect the crowds, who had all turned out in spite of the problems of the preceding week

Of all the displays in 1993, none attracted more media coverage than Fairford, as a result of the collision between two Russian MiG-29s. Countrywide, television viewers were shocked and horrified to see the tragedy re-enacted on the news. However, more staggering than the actual collision was the fact that no-one was seriously injured, which was quite remarkable considering that one of the aircraft fell just outside a village, and the other landed a matter of yards away from a group of spectators, and directly in line with, but a few hundred yards short of the aircrew enclosure. Although I am sure a number of individuals would have welcomed an end to the flying at that point, for the thousands of spectators who had paid their entrance money, such a decision would have been a bitter disappointment. From a pilot's point of view, this accident left me feeling a little like I had fallen off a horse – my confidence had taken a knock, and the best thing I could do was to immediately get back in the saddle, rather than prolong the agony by waiting for another day.

I was programmed to perform 45 minutes after the crash, and despite feeling rather more conscious than usual of the risks involved, was keen to fly. As I taxied out for my display, I could not help noticing the hive of activity still sur-

RIGHT: The last UK show on the calendar provided Rob with a mind focusing incident that could have caused serious damage to his jet. RAF Newton, in Nottinghamshire, is home to both the Bulldog-equipped East Midlands UAS and the Chipmunks of No 7 Air Experience Flight. The facility boasts a reasonable length grass strip eminently suitable for Harrier GR.5/7 operations, or so it was thought. Winter arrived early in the Midlands, and during the week leading up to the Battle of Britain Families Day, Newton was thoroughly soaked on several occasions. The Harrier weighs at least as much as 13 Chipmunks dripping wet, so the problems the pilot could face with the jet sinking on damp ground upon landing are plainly obvious.
Although the No 20(R) Sqn groundcrew performed the standard penetrometer tests prior to declaring the airfield suitable for Harrier ops, it seems that the readings taken by the machine were a little unreliable. After an uneventful arrival and pre-display refuelling, Rob taxied out to commence his routine and his jet promptly began to sink. This was due primarily to the additional 2000 lbs of fuel that had been added for his display. Rob increased the power, thus keeping the aircraft rolling, and fortunately the ground was just firm enough to prevent a 'bog in'. He drove his courtesy Granada (provided along with a Scorpio and a Transit by *Thrifty* and *Budget*) onto the airfield the following day to survey the damage

rounding the smoking wreckage, but once airborne, I was far too busy to think about other things. After the display, with another successful routine behind me, I was able to consider the events of the day in a more balanced, less emotional manner. Although disturbing, aircraft crashes are an unfortunate fact of life, and for the other display pilots, the misfortune of the Russians emphasised the importance of stringent flight safety rules, and served as a reminder that there is no room for complacency.

By the end of the UK season, I had flown 53 displays which, together with over 30 practices, amounted to 14 hours of 'stunting and bunting'. Transiting from one end of the country to the other had clocked up 20,000 miles and accounted for a further 50 hours in the cockpit. Frequent cloud bases below 5000 ft had resulted in the 'rolling show' being flown at most venues, but very low cloud bases had necessitated use of the V/STOL sequence on four occasions – a sad reflection on the summer of 1993.

As the discerning spectator will have noticed, my displays were not confined to one aircraft. In fact 11 of the OCU's GR.5s and 7s were used during the season. This was a deliberate policy designed to prevent any one aircraft from suffer-

ing excessive engine and airframe wear, instead enabling the fatigue to be spread across the fleet. As far as displaying is concerned, there is little difference between the two marks of Harrier. The GR.5 is lighter and so has a slightly greater performance margin, increasing its manoeuvrability in jet-borne flight. However, the GR.7, being the RAF's most recent purchase and not having previously displayed on the UK circuit, is what the enthusiast prefers to see. For this reason, I attempted to take one of each mark on most weekends, electing to fly the GR.7 on all but the warmest days when the GR.5's lighter weight helped to compensate for the reduced engine performance resulting from the higher temperatures.

As the last weekend of September drew near, it seemed that my career as a display pilot had come to an end. Although other fast jet crews tend to perform for two consecutive seasons, for the last few years at least the Harrier pilot has only done the business for one season. I was, therefore, both pleased and surprised to hear that I was to perform in 1994, and almost in the same breath that I would be flying at the Dubai Airshow at the beginning of November. It seemed as though my life as a display pilot was only just beginning. □

A WEEKEND OUTING

VENUES for air displays range in size from the sprawling 10,000 ft concrete runways at RAF stations like Fairford and Mildenhall, to small mown fields like Shoreham and Shuttleworth, both of which boast strips that are less than a quarter of the length of those at modern military bases. The size of the runway also usually dictates the capacity of the venue, organisers blessed with over a mile of black top spreading the attending masses along the length of the aerial 'stage'.

Part and parcel of a lengthy runway is an equally impressive airfield perimeter which is usually covered in taxyways, hardstanding, fuel and ammunition dumps, Hardened Aircraft Shelters (HASs) and accommodation blocks. Virtually all of this space is available for the pilot to perform his routine in, and at some of the largest stations in Britain the more agile fast jets need not cross the base perimeter track at all during their display!

Rob has flown his Harrier GR.5/7 at virtually every venue on the airshow circuit in 1993, entertaining crowds across the British Isles. Due to his aircraft's unique handling characteristics, he has had the opportunity to display his talents on a far wider 'stage' than that available to other RAF fast jet pilots flying conventional aircraft. This was perhaps best illustrated during a sunny weekend in early September 1993 when on consecutive days he operated out of small grass airfields – try doing that in a Tornado or Jaguar.

Although separated by a handful of home counties, and the sprawling sea of humanity that is London, the grass airfields at Shoreham, in Sussex, and Old Warden, in Bedfordshire, are remarkably similar in size. Both offer good flat surfaces for flying civil types on, the runways stretching out for just over 2000 ft. Carefully tendered taxyways connect the grass strips with the limited hangarage facilities at both fields, Shoreham boasting more in the way of permanent structures because of its larger size and general aviation role. The latter airfield also possesses a short tarmac strip.

As the Harrier was designed specifically to operate from dispersed sites along the NATO frontline, both Shoreham and Old Warden

BELOW: During the first weekend in September Rob had the unique experience of operating from grass strips on consecutive days at different airshows. The first of these 'lawn' events was held at Shoreham Airport, in Sussex, when No 20(R) Sqn was asked at the last minute to fill a display slot originally allocated to No 1(F) Sqn who, because of operational commitments overseas, could not attend. Scheduled to open the Manston show the following morning anyway, Rob was more than happy to step into the breech and show off the Harrier's unique capabilities to an appreciative crowd a few miles further along the coast. Surprisingly for September the weather was dry, and the GR.7 kicked up quite a dust storm performing its RVL bounce (Photo by C J Wallace)

BELOW: After a short 30-minute flight around the outskirts of Greater London and across Essex the Harriers arrived over Old Warden. Following staggered 5g breaks into the pattern, both pilots performed textbook rough field landings that used barely half of the aerodrome's beautifully undulating 2000-ft. grass strip. Despite the pilots leaving the right amount of separation between recoveries in an effort to avoid any FOD problems, Rob's aircraft nevertheless suffered alarming damage to its ventral tail fin and port taileron when a concrete threshold marker took to the air as a result of the blast from the four nozzle jets, which are directed almost vertically downwards during the landing phase. Still wearing their g-suits, Rob and Mike listen intently to their squadron boss, Wg Cdr Harper, as he explains what happened (Photo by Tony Holmes)

ABOVE: Anxious to find out exactly what had dented his formerly intact GR.7, Rob jumped aboard the Shuttleworth Collection's Land Rover fire engine and trundled across the grass to the threshold, where an eagle-eyed marshall had found the offending slab. Still wearing his g-suit, and bearing the pressure marks of his oxygen mask across his cheeks, our intrepid display pilot gets to grips with the lump of Blue Circle's finest that minutes before had tried to cripple his GR.7 (Photo by Tony Holmes)

seemed perfectly suited to host the RAF's V/STOL combat aircraft. However, before the pilot can pitch up and land his multi-million pound jet on the green grass, several important factors need to be taken into account. Was the airfield itself firm enough to take 19,000 lbs of steaming fast jet?; could the Harrier be safely refuelled on the site?; and where was the closest

paved diversionary runway in case of rain?

Once these questions had been satisfactorily answered, Rob had to then tailor his flying display to fit into the airspace avilable over and around the strips. Prior to his impressing the crowd with slick high 'g' turns and hovering manoeuvres, the 'mind focusing' task of safely landing the GR.7 on a surface which left little margin for error had to be performed. Grass landings are flown as a matter of routine up at Wittering, the airfield boasting two 3000-ft long strips onto which a 1500-ft marked section has been laid out. This allows the pilot to accurately gauge the distance it takes to slow down to taxying pace from the initial landing point.

Rob had never flown from either venue before, and on his way down to Manston (he was flying at their open day on the morning of the Shuttleworth Pageant) he made a low, slow, gear and flaps down pass over Old Warden at 100 kts, with his wingman for the weekend, Sqn Ldr Mike Young, right behind him. 'The airfield looked to slope away downhill as we flew through it. I had never set foot on the site before, and although occasionally there is time to go out and do a ground inspection, things were rather hectic that weekend and the fly-by was the only chance I got. I thought to myself as we passed over Old Warden, a) that's downhill, and b) that's bloody short!', Rob explained.

After recovering at Manston and topping up the tanks of both Harriers, the pilots flew the short trip along the coast to Shoreham, where a no-nonsense landing was safely performed on the airfield's tarmac runway – the Sussex strip is slightly less undulating and a touch longer than Old Warden, thus making Rob and Mike's task a little easier. After preparing the display jet, Rob duly performed for the small, but appreciative,

TOP LEFT: Rob and Mike were again blessed with ideal air display weather on the Sunday, and after successfully completing the opening routine for the Manston show at midday, the pair enjoyed a quick sandwich and a cup of tea and then made tracks for Bedfordshire. After a long taxy out to the threshold, and a quick final check of the aircrafts' systems through a brief consultation with the HUD symbology, Mike lead the two-ship onto the wide (and very long) runway

ABOVE: As a result of the landing escapade, Rob prepared GR.5 ZD345 for action as his display aircraft for the afternoon's Military Air Pageant. The groundcrew worked feverishly to prepare the jet for its 1510 slot, removing the baggage pod from the centre-fuselage hardpoint, filling the water tank and topping up the fuel. A total of 3000 lbs of Avtur was poured into the GR.5's capacious fuselage and overwing tanks in a matter of minutes by the high-pressure pump fitted to the Scammell. Meanwhile overhead the show goes on as an Extra 230 pulls out of a tight loop (Photo by Tony Holmes)

ABOVE: Only at Shuttleworth could you find such a deliciously wide selection of aircraft that represent virtually the full gamut of powered flight from its inception 91 years ago. This view was taken from Old Warden's modest control tower, and features just a slice of the types that performed for a bumper crowd on 5 September. In the foreground, from left to right, are a Chipmunk T.1, a Hucks starter, an English Electric Wren, a Gloster Gladiator, a Hawker Hind, an LVG CVI, an SE.5a and a Bristol Fighter (Photo by Tony Holmes)

RIGHT: Posing for a unique photograph, two of Hawker's classic 'strike' aircraft sit side by side on the lush green Old Warden lawn. Separated by 60 years in terms of design philosophy, both the Hind and the Harrier were nevertheless built with the same job in mind – bombing enemy targets. Piloting the priceless Hawker biplane on this occasion was Andy Sephton, a former RAF Harrier mate from the late 1980s, who now works for British Aerospace as a test pilot at their Filton plant near Bristol. Aside from throwing the Hind about in exuberant fashion, Andy also flies most of the Collection's other biplane types (Photo by Tony Holmes)

crowd at Shoreham Airport. On this occasion, No 20(R) Sqn were filling in for fellow-Wittering Harrier operators No 1(F) Sqn who, because of historical ties with the town, annually perform a display over the airfield. However, due to operational commitments, the 'Fighting First' could not spare a jet in 1993, so No 20 stepped into the breech – Rob was only given permission to fly his display from Shoreham by the AOC on the day before the actual event!

Both jets returned to Manston for the night, and Rob performed his display once again the following day as the opening routine at the air station's open day. Operating from Manston could not have provided a greater contrast with what lay in store for the pilot at his next venue later in the day – the RAF station in Kent is the south east diversionary field for commercial jets unable to land at Heathrow, Gatwick or Stansted. Not only

does it possess one of the longest paved strips in the country – over 10,000 ft – it also boasts one of the widest, its concrete run-off areas on either side of the main strip in effect creating a three-lane runway.

The display GR.7 was quickly turned around by the dedicated No 20(R) Sqn groundcrew, the aircraft's internal fuel supply being replenished and the demineralised water injection tank refilled. After a leisurely bite to eat, both pilots walked out to their jets, breezed through the pre-flights and departed Manston at 1330. Time on target at Old Warden was 1400, their arrival in the pattern over the airfield signalling the start of the flying at the 1993 Shuttleworth Military Air Pageant. As is always the case throughout the season, Rob had already ensured that a suitable diversionary runway was available in the local area should a problem arise at Old Warden

ABOVE: A confident wave to the crowd as Rob taxies along the runway to the threshold prior to launching into his display. The groundcrew carefully examined the surface at Old Warden for potholes prior to the Harriers' arrival as the airstrip is notorious as the mole capital of Bedfordshire! The physical size of the location was also scrutinised to ensure that Rob could safely turn the jet around at the top of the runway without his outriggers disappearing into uncharted territory *(Photo by Tony Holmes)*

ABOVE RIGHT: Brief pre-flight checks completed, Rob pushes the throttle forward to the stops. The instant acceleration presses him firmly back into his ejection seat, the Pegasus taking just a fraction over four seconds to push the Harrier through the 100-kt barrier. The flaps automatically schedule to 62° as the nozzles are rotated downwards. The former work in conjunction with the distinctive Lift Improvement Devices (LIDs) to trap some of the ground-reflected nozzle exhaust expelled by the Mk105 engine, and propel the jet into the sky *(Photo by Air Portraits)*

that caused the strip to be closed for any period of time.

'We bridged up Cranfield as a 'div', and we went and had a look at it just before we came into Old Warden. Our flight up from Manston was performed at 2000 ft and 360 kts. Once we were in the area, I called up Cranfield and told them that we may have to use their runway in a minute. They handle a lot of 'civvie' traffic on a weekend, and this brief warning gave them time to temporarily clear their pattern of light aircraft. I spotted Old Warden and led Mike down to the briefed height for a tight two-ship run in over the airfield.

'We then broke into the pattern for landing, staggering our approaches so as to remove any chance of Mike suffering a FOD problem with debris kicked up from my RVL. Landing both here and at Shoreham had been our main concern

for the whole weekend, the little light bulbs in the back of your mind coming on and the hairs on your neck bristling to suggest that you could have some fun on recovery. Obviously you can go around again, but that's not the aim in life.'

To help the new-generation GR.5/7 cope with rough field operations, the aircraft is fitted with a highly sophisticated, but equally sensitive, Dunlop anti-skid system which operates rather differently from the device found in the old GR.3.

'You could RVL a GR.3 into Old Warden at about the same speed as a GR.5, but the older jet has a more effective anti-skid system. We had all been used to stopping in the GR.3 by simply jumping on the brakes, and letting the anti-skid system do the rest. In the GR.5/7, although the braking technique remains the same, it feels as though nothing is happening – the anti-skid sys-

tem is just too sensitive! Both pilots and engineers have noted this problem.

'If the anti-skid system is switched off in the jet, you are now left with your feet acting as the brakes and the Dunlop multi-disc carbon brakes possess considerable 'bite' in the manual mode, so you could easily pop the tyres if you are a little heavy with their application. Certainly on tarmac, if you jumped on the brakes even at 15 kts you would blow-out the tyres. Occasionally on the OCU course, the students block the runway, having blown tyres due to switching the anti-skid system off too soon!'

Rob landed in a shower of dirt on the lush green strip and firmly applied the brakes. He immediately felt the GR.7 slowing up, its forward momentum being suitably impeded so as to stop him well before the grass hedge at the end of the runway. In fact, he had slowed to taxying speed before he reached the 04 runway intersection with the downhill strip.

His landing speed had been calculated to the knot, experience over the years having taught Harrier pilots that a speed of 55 kts is ideal for minimizing the dangers of FOD ingestion on grass. 'A normal clean strip landing is 50 kts, but 55 kts is the recommended speed for grass. If you landed even a couple of knots slower you would see the dust cloud that is kicked up on landing being sucked into the intakes.'

Despite the landing being performed as per the textbook, and the aircraft stopping well before the hedgerow, the Harrier still suffered external damage due to debris being kicked up by the jet nozzles. Most grass strips have their thresholds marked out with painted concrete markers, or 'flags', which are sunken into the ground and clearly visible at medium altitude or on approach to landing.

Old Warden's markers had become loose during the dry spell in late August as the ground lost its moisture, and when Rob let down directly over the hedge onto the mown strip, the combined jet blast and vectored thrust cushion of hot air which is trapped beneath the Harrier lifted one of the concrete slabs and slammed it into the ventral tail fin. From there it shot off into the port taileron, the resulting damage being a badly cracked tail fairing and a less than aerodynamic finish to the flying surface. Rob had felt nothing during the landing and was only made aware of the damage by the groundcrew after the jet had taxied in and shut down.

He immediately feared that he might have collided with a light aircraft during the transit up from Manston, but his fears were soon allayed by a Shuttleworth marshaller who had seen the offending object spat out from behind the GR.7 when it touched down. A relieved Rob passed on the news to his boss, Wg Cdr Harper, who, rather ironically, was viewing his flight lieutenant's weekend employment for the second time in the season! This was also the only damage incurred by the Display Team throughout 1993.

The GR.7 was immediately ruled out as the afternoon's display aircraft because the carbon-fibre body work that was damaged upon landing could have been torn even further by the high 'g' stresses absorbed by the airframe during Rob's ten-minute routine – in fact, the ventral fin was 'speed taped' by the turnaround crew, although the tape subsequently blew off prior to take-off! Back at base, both the taileron and the fin were eventually replaced by the squadron engineers.

The ground support team now came into their own in the hour between the Harriers' arriving and Rob flying his display. Kitted out in smart black overalls similar to those worn by the pilots, the four-man crew from No 20(R) Sqn had arrived at Old Warden in the team Sherpa about an hour and a half before their jets pitched up. 'The troops arrive in plenty of time to make sure the site is tidy, that there are no pot holes to taxy into, and that there is enough room for me

TOP LEFT: Within seconds the Harrier is airborne. Rob quickly raises the main gear and outriggers, leaving the flaps to retract automatically according to the airspeed and AoA. The nozzles have already returned to a near-horizontal position, making full use of the 21,000 lbs of thrust available. Old Warden is one of the smallest venues at which the Harrier will display in the season, and this dramatic shot clearly shows its snug confines (*Photo by Air Portraits*)

TOP: Captured seconds after the RVL bounce, the pilot retracts the undercarriage into the fuselage. The jet's 'barn door' flaps and drooping ailerons are clearly visible from this angle (*Photo by Tony Holmes*)

LEFT: Rapturous applause from the 20,000-strong crowd greeted Rob as he climbed out of the creaking and hissing GR.5 following his awesome performance. The strain of the display shows in his face, the distinctive oxygen mask pressure mark synonymous with the fast jet pilot being clearly visible. RAF doctors have equated a high-g ten-minute display with an hour-long tactical mission in terms of heart-beat rate and fatigue *(Photo by Tony Holmes)*

ABOVE: The deceleration and transition to V/STOL flight completed, the final phase of bows, turns and a reverse 'back up' commences over crowd centre. This sequence usually brings the biggest cheer from the crowd as the jet is seemingly within touching distance for almost two minutes. The major drawback of this phase of the display is the heavy fuel consumption *(Photo by Tony Holmes)*

to be safely marshalled around in. They help me keep out of trouble, particularly at a place like this', Rob explained.

The GR.7 had been assigned to perform all the flying that weekend, but circumstances dictated that the supporting GR.5 now had to serve as Rob's display jet. The aircraft had flown into Old Warden fitted with a baggage pod on the centreline pylon, and this had to be swiftly removed, the tanks topped up with 3000 lbs of fuel and the water injection system replenished. Water injection is used on every display, the 50-gal (500-lb) supply usually running out after a minute and a half. The boost it provides is used at the pilot's discretion, and on a hot day it can be vital during the early stages of the routine when the Harrier can feel a little lethargic due to its fuel load. Engine wear is also reduced by its use, thereby prolonging the life of the hard-worked Pegasus powerplant.

Whilst the crew prepared the jet externally, Rob was more concerned about the state of his aircraft from within the cockpit. 'The inertial navigation system (INS) in the GR.7 that I was originally supposed to fly is activated by the aircraft's built-in auxiliary power unit, and takes about seven minutes to align itself with its surroundings. So if you fire it up prior to performing your walkaround of the jet, by the time you jump

in and complete your checks, the INS is ready, you're ready and you simply spool up the engine, and off you go. That is how I usually work out my display timing as well, commencing my count-down from the moment I lean into the cockpit and activate the INS.

'However, at Old Warden as I strode out to the GR.5 I could see that it was already time to climb in and fire up the engine, yet the crew had not yet taken the baggage pod off. By this stage I would normally have finished my walkaround, signed the books acknowledging my satisfaction with the state of the jet and jumped in. To make matters worse I then found out that the INS was engine align only in the 'new' display jet, which means that you have to get the powerplant running before you can activate the system, and then wait the mandatory seven minutes!

'At this point I thought that there was no way I would make my slot, which is the last thing you want, but as it turned out it translation started, the INS responding to the activation of the auxiliary power unit, so I was alright.'

THE DISPLAY

Now strapped in, and with the Pegasus bellowing out its screeching tone, Rob checked his flying surfaces for freedom of movement, and satisfied as to the health of his jet, waved the chocks away.

ABOVE: Whilst the Toyota Team in their Pitts S.2B Specials and Extra 230 thrill the crowd with daring deeds overhead, Rob and Sgt Forrester get to grips with ZD345's Form 700 files. The pilot's flight notes, written on his kneepad, are meticulously transferred to the aircraft log, allowing checks to be made at any stage in the jet's life on such things as engine wear, avionics reliability and the general condition of the airframe *(Photo by Tony Holmes)*

The Harrier lurched forward as he released the brakes and opened the throttle ever so slightly. With the engine idling at 25 per cent of its available rpm, the GR.5 moved quickly across the grass away from the crowdline, its nose lolling up and down as the pilot dabbed on the brakes to check their operability. 'The Harrier is usually taxied with the nozzles located in the 60° position to stop the aircraft from 'running away', but with the braking action of the rough grass, I left the nozzles aft.

'I moved away from the crowd as quickly as possible because of the engine noise, which is particularly bad in front of the jet. When you've got 'mates' displaying in small aircraft where the engine noise is half the appeal, it is sensible to hold as far away from the crowd as possible.'

When his time came to perform his routine Rob taxied gingerly along the length of old Warden's main runway and swung his jet around into wind at the extreme threshold of the strip, thus giving the aircraft the full length of the 'lawn' in which to take-off.

Lined-up with brakes on, he begun a frantic routine of hand movements within the cockpit that had been carried out so many times before that they were now almost instinctive. The Hawker Hind and Gloster Gladiator that had performed immediately prior to the GR.5 now trundled off the taxyway, and Rob was cleared to launch. The aircraft's engine noise increased in pitch as the pilot opened the throttle to 55 per cent rpm. Everything was functioning correctly, and the figures in Rob's HUD were exactly as they should be. Time to roll.

The routine began the milli-second Rob was airborne, the undercarriage being quickly cycled away and the jet reefed into a sharp turn to the right of the strip. This was followed by a massive positive 'g' 35° pitch up and accelerating climb, the pilot straining against the compression of this eye-watering manoeuvre. Whilst all of this was

BELOW: The cast and crew of the Harrier Display Team at Shuttleworth on 5 September. From left to right: Junior Tech Allsop; Sgt Forrester; Cpl Osler; Flt Lt Lea; Senior Aircraftsman Robertson; Junior Tech McKie; and Sqn Ldr Young. All the groundcrew hail from No 20(R) Sqn and work five days a week on the unit's Harrier force at Wittering. Support of the 'weekend' flying is purely voluntary *(Photo by Tony Holmes)*

ABOVE: Locations don't come much more rural than Shuttleworth, as emphasised by this view. The seemingly elongated 'big wing' on the Harrier is one the largest single carbon-fibre composite components built into any fast jet, and it boasts a detachable top skin to facilitate ease of access for maintenance and inspection purposes. The proliferation of underwing stores pylons on the jet are also graphically illustrated from this angle *(Photo by Tony Holmes)*

going on, Rob was also tuned into the radio, listening intently to the tower who were instructing the pilot of a light aircraft holding off to the north east of the airfield to immediately leave the area. The weekend pilot's full compliance with this request was crucial as in a couple of minutes time Rob was planning to turn around and pull up in that very spot following his crowd passes!

He also spotted a glider away to the right of Old Warden soon after commencing his routine, which he also had to keep a firm eye on throughout the display. 'It concentrates the mind when aircraft approach your display area. Although he never got closer than a mile, it is something you do not want to be constantly thinking about when you are turning and banking during the performance. After every manoeuvre you have to re-check his position!' Rob exclaimed.

The 1993 GR.5/7 display consisted of seven distinctive parts, each of which flowed into the next so as to give the crowd ten minutes of exhilerating entertainment. Rob's performances varied slightly depending on the weather and the venue. At the Shuttleworth Pageant, he was forced to fly a slightly modified derivation of his rolling display because of the medium level cloud base, and to suit the venue's unusual layout.

Through the course of the airshow season in the UK, which lasts between May and October, Rob will have flown his routine over 100 times. Of all those performances he rated Shuttleworth as one of the hardest. 'The pageant was the most challenging flying I've encountered this summer

in terms of take-off and landing restrictions due to airfield size. Another factor that has to be taken into account at shows like this is that the airfield itself is not well defined, being surrounded by trees on all sides.

'If you look back at any concrete runway having flown a turn, or roll, it is still clearly there. Here, it is seemingly always behind you, and you have quickly passed the end of the strip before you even know it. You really need to pick up features on the extended centreline in both directions to pull around and aim at until you can actually see the runway again.'

Following a typically professional routine, which thoroughly wrung the cobwebs out of the 'spare jet', Rob performed a text book rough-field landing and taxied back to the crowdline. As he climbed out of the creaking and hissing GR.5, now firmly chocked and receiving attention from the clutch of groundcrew, the pilot was welcomed back to terra firma by a standing ovation from the 20,000-strong crowd, which, although numerically not the largest gathering he had performed for in 1993, was far and away the most appreciative.

Now all that needed to be done was for the Form 700 maintenance log to be filled out by the pilot and his chief tech, and the g-suit to be removed. After that, Rob could head off for a well deserved cup of tea. 'It's exhausting performing these routines. You land with your throat as dry as dust. Unfortunately, at a lot of venues there is only time to refuel and then jump back in the jet

RIGHT: A pilot's eye view of the Old Warden strip – not overly long is it! The seemingly limitless power of the Pegasus allows the GR.7 to easily cope with air strips of this type

BELOW RIGHT: Having left Old Warden, the team proceeded to Birmingham International Airport, which was to be the starting point for an unusual sortie the following day. Flanked by European automotive exotica, Mike and Rob pose with the Allied Dunbar Eagle and company employees Peter Jones and Nick Browning at RAF Lyneham following the brief flight from the Midlands. Both gentlemen had just completed a dash to the top of the Empire State Building in New York and back within 24 hours, a feat which raised £25,000 for charity. The Harrier Display Team did their bit by flying the 'eagle' on its last stage from Birmingham to Lyneham

LEFT: Rob checks the progress of his wingman whilst Senior Aircraftsman Robertson secures the undernose access panel latches. The distinctive twin-prong antennae affixed to the jet's proboscis serve as the forward hemisphere receivers for the jet's Marconi Defence Systems Zeus ECM kit. The most advanced equipment of its kind currently fitted to any RAF jet, the Zeus was delayed in its development phase for so long that all GR.5s entered service without it. Above the prongs is the Hughes ASB-19(V)-2 Angle Rate Bombing Sight, which can operate in conjunction with laser – and TV – guided ordnance for precision attacks. The tell-tale GR.7 bulge on the upper nose contains a GEC Sensors FLIR (forward looking infrared) *(Photo by Tony Holmes)*

and head off for the next appointment. Shuttleworth, however, is the business, as you are treated as a guest, unlike at a lot of the bigger events, and you are close enough to the crowd to really feel their appreciation at the end of a well-flown routine. The Shoreham/Shuttleworth weekend was definitely one of the most enjoyable for me in 1993.

'In terms of the routines and transiting from one venue to another they were fairly typical of how each weekend was spent in the summer. I would usually fly three shows over a two-day period, although on the rare occasion during busy weekends I actually flew four.

'The RAF closely monitor my calender as the strain and exertion of a ten-minute display is roughly equitable to an hour-long tactical sortie in terms of heartbeats and fatigue. They don't

take the attitude that because you have only flown 30 minutes of display flying today, you can go out and do another couple of hours in the cockpit later on a training or tactical mission. Basically, four shows, with a couple of transits, is your lot for the weekend.'

His 'lot' for the weekend entertained thousands at three separate venues in the south east of England, and hopefully gave the the taxpayer a better understanding of the capilities of the modern RAF.

The Harrier has always been the air force's trump Public Relations card ever since it first entered service at Wittering over 25 years ago, and with pilots of the calibre of Rob Lea displaying the new-generation jet to its fullest ability, it will remain a firm favourite well into the next century.

PART TIME QFI

'DON'T like Mondays', is probably a familiar feeling amongst display pilots. Up early. Fighting with display organisers for a take-off slot. Searching for a fire tender that will allow you to start the engine. Returning to your friendly home base, often quite fatigued from the weekend's events, to be met by your bright-eyed and rested work mates, eager to begin their week's flying.

'Hello stranger', 'paying us a visit?' and 'part time QFI' were familiar greetings. Even the engineers joined in on the banter, asking me 'Could I remember how to strap into a T.4?' as I walked out through the line hut to give an instructional sortie.

The facts of the matter were that disappearing after lunch on a Friday, re-appearing on the Monday morning, and taking a day off mid-week, meant that I was only available to instruct for just over half of the normal working week, and much of my time was spent preparing for the coming weekend. From my point of view, the day off was essential to enable me to 'erect my gyros' and prevent the garden from resembling a field, but it significantly increased the workload of the other members of staff. However, the OCU has coped with this burden admirably over the years, but the comments served to remind me that my absence had been noted.

The OCU consists of two squadron: 'B' and 'A'. Fundamentally, B Sqn staff teach conversion onto the T.4 and GR.7, circuit work, instrument flying, V/STOL, air combat and low-level navi-

gation. The students then move onto A Sqn, learning simulated attack profiles, tactical formation flying and weaponry. Whilst at Wittering, as one of the six B Sqn instructors I was responsible for helping to teach the first half of the OCU syllabus.

Like all courses, the OCU begins with a period of ground school, the first taste lasting just over a week and serving to introduce the systems and cockpit layout of the T.4. Unlike the basic and advanced flying training schools, there are no dedicated ground school staff at the OCU. Therefore we, the 'flying' instructors, take to the classroom for a couple of hours each day to attempt to bring the systems to life. The students usually find ground school too short to become frustrating, the week barely providing enough

RIGHT: Until late 1991 all simulator sorties were flown at one of two US Marine Corps base – Yuma or Cherry Point. It was not until almost three years after the first GR.5s arrived at Wittering that the Link-Miles Harrier Full Mission Simulator 'launched' on its first sortie. A total of eight detailed trips are 'flown' by students over a period of ten days, covering general handling and instrument flying, as well as rudimentary emergency procedures. Once the initial 'sim' work has been successfully completed, students then move on to the 'real thing'. In this dramatic photograph, the pupil is decelerating to the hover as he approaches the stern of a computer-generated HMS _Invincible_

BELOW: The old and the very new sit side by side on the Wittering ramp. The family resemblance between the stretched twin and its young cousins is readily apparent from this angle, although the enlarged wing area of the GR.7s contrasts with the almost inadequate looking flying surface of the T.4. The Laarbruch-based Harriers were operating from Wittering to enable them to utilise the low-level ranges in Norfolk in preparation for their deployment to Turkey as part of _Operation Warden_

time for them to square away the checks and emergency drills prior to their first flight. The ground school phase can be quite interesting for the staff because with the students confined to the classroom, we are able to fly our own tactical sorties, thus getting plenty of 'hands on time' when not teaching systems.

And then the fun begins, as the students embark on a series of 14 sorties flown from the front of a T.4, with one of the B Sqn staff hovering over the controls to the rear. With its cramped, high mounted cockpit, enormous array of instruments (including for most their first taste of a head-up display), impressive acceleration and abnormal handling characteristics, the Harrier proves a handful for any pilot to begin with.

On the first sortie, the students initially leave the nozzles aft, so that they can examine the conventional handling characteristics of the aircraft. Returning to the circuit, the remainder of the sortie is spent coming to terms with the most straight forward form of Harrier approach, the 60° nozzle slow landing. This approach is flown using 20° of nozzles downwind (enabling the RCVs to be checked), 40° in the turn and 60° for the approach. With increasing nozzle angles, the amount of lift provided by engine thrust rises, reducing the wing lift contribution, and enabling the jet to fly at lower speed.

This 'Standard Circuit' benefits from a lower touchdown speed and therefore a shorter landing roll than a conventional circuit which is used only in case of emergency. As fuel weight, configuration and nozzle angle all significantly affect the stall speed, students are taught to rely on angle of attack rather than airspeed, a transition that comes more easily to some than others.

The aspect of this sortie that the students find the most difficult is the landing and braking phase. Unlike every other aircraft that they have flown to date, the Harrier is not flared onto the runway, but must instead be held in a horizontal attitude. Also the wings must be level at touchdown to avoid damaging the relatively fragile outriggers. Most importantly, the ingrained instinct of closing the throttle just prior to touchdown must be overcome, for with such a large proportion of the lift being provided by jet thrust, any such tendencies result in a very firm landing.

Once on the ground, stopping is rather more complicated than just standing on the brakes. On touchdown, the throttle must be slammed to idle to prevent a power bounce, nose-wheel steering is engaged by depressing a lever on the control column, and the nozzle lever is moved back and lifted over a gate into the braking position. With the nozzles deflected, the reaction controls are activated, and so to prevent foreign objects from

RIGHT: Plt Off Jules Hatton-Ward is helped with his straps by SACW Komorowska at the beginning of a handling sortie in the squadron's sole T.4A – it differs from the T.4 in that it lacks the laser rangefinder and marked target seeker (LRMTS) nose modification. The long-course conversion lasts six months and sees a pilot officer, fresh from a TWU, graduate with 83 hours of Harrier flying in his log book. 'Retread' pilots from other fast jet communities are also catered for by the OCU. The well-worn state of the cockpit and canopy sills on this jet bear testament to the heavy usage of the 'twin-stick' fleet

BELOW RIGHT: Full recognition as a front-line Harrier pilot is the 'gold' at the end of Wittering's rainbow for student pilots

RIGHT: Amongst the hardest worked aircraft in the RAF, the handful of T.4s at Wittering will be forced to soldier on with the OCU for at least another three years whilst British Aerospace build their replacements in the form of 14 Harrier T.10s. The two-seaters are used primarily to provide students with hands-on experience of V/STOL flight, under the close scrutiny of a QFI. Unfortunately, their use as a lead-in tool for the GR.5/7 is limited to basic hovering and circuit work as the older jet's systems and general handling differ dramatically from the new breed of Harrier. Wearing the OC's pennant below the cockpit, this T.4 is having its inertial navigation system (INS) aligned on external power prior to launch. Smiling for the camera as she removes the push-in starboard intake cover is Senior Aircraftswoman (SACW) Pattenden

being blown from the runway into the enormous engine intakes, the nose reaction control must be shut before power is applied. This is achieved by motoring the pitch trim forward of the neutral setting. Checking nozzle and trim positions, power is then increased to 60 per cent, providing engine braking down to 60 kts, at which point the throttle is closed, nozzles are returned to less than 60° and normal wheel braking commences.

If the brakes are applied at the same time as reverse thrust is being used, the tyres will burst. Getting this procedure out of sequence can prove disastrous, and during my short time on the OCU, I have seen all sorts of interesting techniques being attempted. Needless to say, the instructor needs to be particularly vigilant if he is to provide timely corrections and advice.

The student's second trip is a consolidation of the first, after which, until up to a year ago, they would have gone solo in the single-seat GR.3. Unfortunately, poor serviceability and spares support for the ageing GR.3 fleet have necessitated the withdrawal of the venerable jet from the syllabus. Hence, they are now used only by staff pilots on rare occasions – a sad loss for students, though not for suppliers and engineers, this means that they now have to wait until their GR.7 conversion before going solo.

With conventional handling and 60° nozzle circuits mastered, the syllabus moves onto jet-borne manoeuvring, with a series of three, fifteen-minute hovering sorties. Three thousand pounds of fuel is just enough to enable three vertical take-offs, hovers and vertical landings to be performed before the tanks are empty, and the sortie complete. Though fundamentally the same as the helicopter, the Harrier is heavier, has more momentum and is slower to respond to control inputs when in the hover. A more restricted cockpit view makes assessment of drift more difficult, and this, together with a smaller performance margin, explains why the students find hovering quite demanding to begin with.

Having experienced jetborne and wingborne flight on separate sorties, students now move onto transitions from jetborne to wingborne flight and vice versa. This is the most dangerous aspect of their training because of the problems that can occur if sideslip is allowed to develop. For this reason, the sorties are very carefully briefed and monitored. Also, the complicated interaction of power, attitude, flight path and angle of attack require that the effects of the controls throughout the transition from one extreme of flight to the other are fully understood. With a nozzle lever, as well as the throttle and control column to worry about, there is plenty of potential for mistakes. To keep life as simple as possible during these early sorties, strict wind limits (as low as ten knots) are enforced, the undercarriage is left down and all transitions and jetborne manoeuvres are carried out over a prepared surface.

The 50° nozzle, or 'short take-off' (STO), is the next manoeuvre to be taught on the syllabus. Designed to reduce the length of the take-off run, this is the most popular method of taking to the air in the Harrier. The STO is flown by accelerating to a predetermined speed with the nozzles aft, and then quickly lowering the nozzles to 50° to encourage early lift off. The second half of the manoeuvre is similar to the latter part of an accelerating transition from the hover, in which the nozzles are slowly moved aft to the conventional position as airspeed and wing lift increase.

With nozzles that are capable of moving over a range of 98°, there are an infinite number of ways of taking off and landing in the Harrier. However, with so little experience, the students are taught a limited number of techniques. Landings are restricted to vertical or rolling vertical, 60° nozzle or fixed throttle slow landings, and take-offs are either vertical or STOs.

The last two T.4 sorties are spent instrument flying. These trips are designed merely as an introduction to instruments, and therefore do not culminate in a rating, but serve as a suitable

BELOW: Once a familiar site on Wittering's flightline, the Harrier GR.3 has now all but disappeared from the station – three or four machines are kept airworthy for staff continuation and training, however. The last GR.3s were phased out in the summer of 1993 when poor serviceability rates and a shortage of spares made them unreliable – similar problems are being experienced with the T.4s

conclusion to the T.4 phase. Now the students must convert onto the GR.7.

As there are currently no two-seat GR.7s in service in the RAF, conversion onto the new type must be performed very carefully and under close supervision. To this end, training initially takes the form of one-and-a-half weeks of ground-school in which individuals get to grips with the cockpit layout, instruments, avionic systems and emergencies, before embarking upon a series of eight simulator trips. These sorties are all taught by B Sqn staff, the sequences very closely following the syllabus that the students have just completed in the T.4. This enables them to gain experience in the safe confines of a simulator, before being let loose in the single-seat aircraft. By the end of the simulator phase, the students are fully prepared for their first solo. On this, and many of the subsequent sorties, to enable progress to be assessed and advice given, the instructor takes to the air in another GR.7, chasing or leading the student through the sequence.

ABOVE: Rob endures the adrenalin buzz of low-level training in Wales with a student in the front seat. The poor view afforded the instructor in the T.4 is readily apparent, as is the rather rudimentary nature of the HUD symbology. The latter is quite narrow in the GR.3/T.4 when compared with the GR.5/7, and the pilot can only read information displayed on it if he keeps his head in the central position. Despite its shortcomings, the T.4 is the only training aid that allows the QFIs' to examine the students' performance at first-hand before clearing them to fly the GR.5/7. B (Basic) Sqn relies heavily on the T.4, particularly in the initial phases of conversion when the students log over 15 trips in the jet

ABOVE: A long course student practices close formation work by keeping his T.4 tucked in snugly behind the GR.3 lead jet. The relatively 'pylonless' under-wing area of the early Harrier contrasts markedly with its GR.5/7 replacement, as does the positioning of its outriggers. Despite its vintage, the GR.3 can still outclimb and outpace its replacement, primarily because of its lighter weight and cleaner wing profile

On a number of other flights, however, instruction can be more effectively provided from a vantage point on the ground, so the QFI ventures out in a Land Rover to stand on the grass by the side of a strip, or vertical landing pad, with a portable radio on his back, to watch the students' performance. To improve the quality of the instruction, all take-offs and landings are recorded on video from a safe distance, students occasionally keeping the footage after it has been used for the debrief as a record of their first attempts at V/STOL.

By the end of the 15th trip, the initial conversion is complete. From now on the emphasis moves away from V/STOL onto more operational flying, which includes low-level navigation, tactical formating and air combat.

The key to successful navigation in the GR.7 is making the best use of the mass of available information. Heading and time to the next way-point, groundspeed and a moving map, which provides present position and wind corrected track, all help to make the pilot's life easier if used sensibly. All too often, the wealth of information can confuse the inexperienced operator, increasing rather than easing his workload. A building block approach to use of the kit is employed to familiarise the individual with the Harrier's many

ABOVE: As part of the student's 'ConvEx' (conversion exercise) phase he will concentrate on polishing his V/STOL skills by flying short sorties of 20 minutes duration in the Wittering circuit. Here, a pilot prepares to vertically land on the base's 'Vigo pad', which is simply a concrete surface partially surrounded by trees at the western end of Wittering's runway. This exercise prepares the student for in-theatre operations, where he will have to land on a 75 ft² 'Mexe pad' placed in a tree clearing near a field site. The sortie is flown under the watchful gaze of an instructor equipped with a radio, who stands to one side of the pad. As a precaution, the station fire brigade are always in attendance when a 'Vigo pad' flight is being performed – very reassuring!

ABOVE: On the first few sorties in the Harrier GR.7, the student is shadowed by a QFI in a similar jet to ensure that his pupil is not overwhelmed by the new aeroplane and cockpit layout. No 20(R) Sqn usually boasts about a dozen instructors at any one time, which are split evenly between A and B Sqns. The QFIs all serve with the latter, whilst the Qualified Weapons Instructors (QWIs) man the former. A long course will usually consists of four to six students, this small number allowing the instructors to personally tutor every pupil. In this photograph, Rob sits and waits whilst his student conducts his final pre-flight checks prior to taxying onto the main runway

ABOVE RIGHT: QFI Flt Lt Pete Woore of B Sqn extricates himself from his GR.5. Logically, A Sqn carry out the post-grad QWI courses, whilst B Sqn fulfil a similar requirement for QFIs and instrument rating examiners

systems, and gradually increase his capability.

To complete their training on B Sqn, the students climb up to medium level to learn the art of combating the Harrier. Made famous by the Falklands campaign, some of the fundamentals of vectoring the thrust in forward flight, or 'Viffing', have been well documented. However, most accounts simplify its use, and fail to address the tactical implications. It is not quite as straight forward as moving the nozzles forward, stopping the aircraft in mid air, and shooting the opponent as he flies by at a rapid rate of knots.

The Harrier will not hover at an altitude of 10,000 ft, and decelerating the aircraft could well solve the aggressor's problems, providing him with a bigger target, and leaving you slow and therefore vulnerable to attack from other aircraft. In reality, the 'braking stop fly through' is just one of a large number of 'Viff' manoeuvres, and is only used as a last resort.

'Viffing' is most effectively used at slower speeds where it produces significantly greater rates of turn without throwing away energy. Also, deflecting the nozzles activates the reaction ducts providing greater control and enabling the aircraft to perform otherwise impossible manoeuvres that can surprise or outwit an opponent.

Combat is perhaps the most popular phase for the students, as they come to realise the potential of the aircraft before moving on to A Sqn to learn low level tactics and weaponry. For the B Sqn staff, a return to the T.4 is in store as four new faces arrive, eager to take up the challenge. ☐

RIGHT: As a QFI, Rob is part of B Sqn, and many of his sorties involve following novice Harrier pilots across the United Kingdom. The OCU also spends a considerable amount of time running post-graduate courses, providing QFI, QWI and Instrument rating examiner qualifications, plus refresher training

BELOW RIGHT: No doubt thanking the fact that they decided to use the covered tow tractor instead of the cabriolet model, a trio of aircraft handlers pull a GR.7 back from the flightline to the shelter of the OCU hangar whilst a summer shower drowns Wittering. With almost two-dozen Harriers on strength, the OCU is easily the largest operator of the jet in the RAF. Due to its size, the squadron also boasts a healthy number of personnel – aside from the 12 instructors (including the 'boss'), the unit controls 24 technicians within the Simulator Flight, plus an Engineering Flight of 150, split between the Aircraft Handling Flight (50) who 'run the flightline', and the Aircraft Rectification Flight (100) who perform jet servicing

OTHER MATES
Tucano T.1, No 3 Flying Training Squadron

Flt Lt Phil Jones

'**W**ELL Phil, you've won the competition. Are you happy to do the season?' These were the Chief Instructors words back in March 1993 at the conclusion of RAF Cranwell's station aerobatics competition. Events had moved pretty quickly during the previous two months, so I confess to giving it a moments thought before replying, 'Yes, I'd be delighted to.'

Prior to those two months, I had not even dreamt of being an aerobatic display pilot. My normal day job is as a flying instructor on No 2 Sqn within No 3 FTS at Cranwell, teaching basic flying to the latest recruits in the Shorts Tucano T.1, and whilst this includes aerobatics instruction, it is a world apart from display flying. As to my previous experience, well few would regard four years on VC10 transport aircraft as an essential pre-requisite for the job, and whilst a similar period on Phantom FGR.2s before that sounds more the ticket, in reality aerobatics were seldom flown in this particular aircraft in an attempt to conserve airframe life.

To find a cause for this desire to fly aerobatics I have to go back further, to summer afternoons skipping university lectures and putting off that studying till the evening to go flying with the University Air Squadron. Thus, it had been 15 years since I had last flown low-level aerobatics, then in the Bulldog T.1 during the inter UAS de Havilland Trophy competition. It's surprising the things you remember though, as I found when I had a recent ride in the Bulldog and could still fly the basic aerobatic manoeuvres, as well as recall numbers such as the revs per minute drop during the magneto checks.

Back to the Tucano though. The run-up to the competition had been short, a note going around inviting applicants just a few months earlier. Before looking at sequence design let's examine our aircraft. The Tucano T.1 is a very

different aerobatic performer compared with its predecessor, the Jet Provost. Turboprop-powered with 1050 SHP, it has a nine second take-off run, a very tight turning circle of 300 m radius, very light controls and better visibility. This is coupled with very rapid engine response, faster roll rate and whilst the normal speed range is lower, this merely serves to keep manoeuvres closer to the crowd. The aircraft's g-limits are +6 to -2.5, and during the sequence I fly to +5.9 and -2.0!

WORK-UPS

Sequence design was done a little in the dark with little help or information save the sequence used by the previous display pilot. Some points are fairly obvious; the rolling manoeuvres need to be along the crowd line and in the centre, looping manoeuvres along the line too, with half cubans to reverse direction. Others were less so; I use a line 45° to the display line for stall turns to present them to the crowd whilst staying close and at the same time reversing direction. The sequence needed to be both balanced and show the aircraft in its best light, as well as obviously staying within its engine and airframe limits. Finally, in order to keep the display tight and the crowd interested the routine had to run for just five minutes.

This was quite a tall order, especially since the practices for the proposed sequence were all initially carried out at above 5000 ft, where the aircraft's performance is different – it rolls quicker and pitches slower and it's difficult to judge the size and positioning of the display relative to a crowd. To give some idea of this, various sequences were drawn out to scale to see how manoeuvres would fit together, and then they were tried out at height. The engine oil limitations required some thought too. The oil system allows a maximum of 15 seconds in the vertical followed by twice that period to recover, before entering the next vertical manoeuvre. This meant more juggling of manoeuvres within the sequence to adhere to this requirement.

I practised at 5000 ft initially, then progressively reduced the minimum height to 500 ft. Each practise was constructively criticised by my supervisor, Rad Greene, and videoed as an aid during the debrief. The first practice at a lower height was always exciting, for despite the needles on the altimeters confirming you had sufficient height to complete a manoeuvre, the ground always looked uncomfortably close. For each manoeuvre I have a minimum or 'gate height' in which to complete it safely, and for the Tucano typical heights are 1800 ft at the top of a looping manoeuvre and 1300 ft pointing straight down after a vertical manoeuvre to guarantee levelling out at 500 ft.

Manoeuvres are never flown at maximum performance as this leaves no margin for error. For instance, after a stall turn the pull commences at 1300 ft, pulling to the light buffet but slackening off as the nose approaches the level attitude to achieve 500 ft.

ABOVE: The Tucano T.1 has been fully integrated into the RAF's training syllabus, as this formation shot confirms. Sandwiched between the photographer's aircraft and the number three in this formation is a Central Flying School Tucano up from RAF Scampton. All air force QFI's are initially trained at the Lincolnshire base, before moving on to the various Flying Training Schools like No 3 FTS, the operatos of the second Tucano in this photograph *(Photo by D J Shepherd)*

ABOVE: Happy with his day's work Phil winds down after a slick display that has seen him push his Tucano close to its g-limits. When not performing in his aircraft, Phil spends his week teaching students as a QFI at Cranwell with No 2 Sqn. Prior to joining Support Command, he served four years in the right-hand seat of a VC10C1 with No 10 Sqn, having earlier in his career completed a tour on Phantom FGR.2s. Despite almost a decade of frontline flying, Phil puts his passion for aerobatics down to his UAS days in Bulldog T.1s!

When performing relative to any ground feature, the biggest factor affecting the sequence is the wind. I tried to design the sequence for a 10-kt wind along the crowd line, but included several manoeuvres and turns that enabled me to cater for the off-crowd or dreaded on-crowd wind.

THE SEQUENCE

After take-off, pre-display checks are carried out, including an inverted check for any loose articles, the last thing you'd want during a display. I start running in towards the crowd with a speed of 180 kts, a good manoeuvring speed which allows me to pull into the height buffet without overstressing. The first manoeuvre is a Derry turn. I then pull to around 60° nose up, roll inverted and push, waiting for 1800 ft before committing nose low in the half cuban.

Still along the crowd line with any drift applied, it's now time for a four-point roll, aiming to achieve the inverted position at 500 ft abeam crowd centre. A 5g turn away through 30°-70°, depending on the wind, positions the aircraft for the first variant of the stall turn, a four-point hesitation. As the aircraft points down, I

look at the wings to make sure I'm vertical, check the crowd line for orientation and wait for the magic 1300 ft figure to appear on the altimeter before I start the pull out.

Rolling underneath at 80 kts for a Canadian break onto the display line, I fly an aileron roll and then pull away for the noddy stall turn. Next, I parallel the line and position the aircraft slightly further away, enabling the crowd to see the square loop without straining (this also helps if there is an on-crowd wind).

The loop starts from 180 kts, with a $5\frac{1}{2}$ g pull to the vertical, held till 120 kts and around 2200 ft, at which point I pull to the inverted attitude, making sure that corrections for drift are made.

I look down for crowd centre and once past it select idle power, airbrake out and pull vertically down, again waiting for 1300 ft. Then it's airbrake in, full power and pull to the light buffet. Next, it's a half Cuban, which allows compensation for wind and positioning, followed by the hard turn away, which precedes the third stall turn variant, the Prince of Wales.

Pulling up from around 180 kts, as soon as the vertical is achieved left rudder is applied to nod 30° to the left, then right rudder to nod right, and finally rudder again left to return to the vertical, with the speed falling rapidly through 100 kts. I apply full stick forward to push over the top, with large inputs of aileron to keep the wings level. A half vertical roll with the engine at idle power and airbrake out gives me a speed of 160 kts for the slow roll along the length of the display axis.

With the Tucano wing the level roll requires considerable attitude changes and large applications of 'top' rudder. The slow speed is maintained as I enter a stall turn left applying full left rudder at 50 kts, but leaving full power on as I need to increase energy for the final manoeuvres. After a half hesitation reverse Cuban with 200 kts positioned exactly over crowd centre, I pull into a tight $5\frac{1}{2}$ g climb for the impressive knife edge loop.

Just past the vertical I apply full aileron to show the aircraft plan view to the crowd, using rudder, plus any along axis wind, to shape the top half of the loop, topping out at around 2500 ft. With the third-quarter of the loop completed, I apply full aileron again before pulling to complete the manoeuvre. The speed is now around 230 kts as I enter the last turn away for a 6g pull to a 360° vertical roll at crowd centre, pushing out at an altitude of just over 3000 ft.

The sequence is now over, but its not the time to relax, with checks and a landing to rapidly complete before the next pilot can display. Each display and venue has been interesting and differ-

RIGHT: Simplicity is the key to a successful basic trainer, and few ab initio aircraft could boast a more ergonomically attractive cockpit than Short's Tucano T.1. All the dials and switches are clearly labelled and easy to read, thus allowing the student to concentrate on his/her flying without having to spend crucial time head down in the cockpit trying to focus on obscure symbology. The angle of attack meter, stopwatch and g-meter are sturdily mounted above the main bank of instruments, almost directly in the pilot's line of vision

ent, with grass runways and sea front displays providing other factors to consider. I've also enjoyed the variation between the large and small shows, civilian and military. For extra spice there have occasionally been overseas events to attend, with the chance to view foreign aerobatic displays in warmer climates.

It's been a great deal of work, but fun none the less and the Tucano itself fits neatly into the airshow programme to show the public and aspiring aviators the first stepping stone that the embryo RAF pilot uses in his or her quest towards a frontline type, be it a Tornado, Hercules, Nimrod or Puma.

Shorts Tucano T.1

Country of Origin: United Kingdom (Brazil)

Type: Tandem two-seat basic trainer

Powerplant: One 1100 shp Garrett TPE331-12B/701A turboprop

Performance: Max speed (at 4850 lb/2200 kg), 320 mph (515 km/h) at 14,000 ft (4270 m), (at 5732 lb/2600 kg), 315 mph (508 km/h) at 12,500 ft (3810 m); econ cruise, 253 mph (407 km/h) at 20,000 ft (6100 m); max initial climb, 3510 ft/min (17.83 m/sec); range (with 30 min reserves), 1082 miles (1742 km) at 25,000 ft (7620 m), (with two 72.6 Imp gal/300 l external tanks), 2073 mls (3355 km)

Weights: Basic empty, 4447 lb (2017 kg); max take-off (aerobatic), 5842 lb (2650 kg), (weapons configuration), 7220 lb (3275 kg)

Status: Brazilian-built prototype flown on 14 February 1986, with first Shorts-built aircraft having flown 30 December 1986. Total of 130 built for the RAF

Dimensions: Span, 37 ft 0 in (11.28 m); length, 32 ft 4¼ in (9.86 m); height, 11 ft 1⅞ in (3.40 m); wing area, 208.07 sq ft (19.33 m²)

HawkT.1A
RAF Valley Standards Flight

Flt Lt Geraint Herbert

IN DECEMBER 1992 I had been flying the Hawk as an instructor for three-and-a-half years and there were no signs of an imminent posting. I felt that I needed a fresh challenge, and displaying the aircraft was exactly what I was looking for. This type of flying was not a new interest as two years earlier I had flown the spare aircraft for that season's display pilot, accompanying him to nearly all of his shows. I had enjoyed the airshow 'party circuit', but mostly wished I was flying instead of drinking!

So, at the start of December I walked into the Chief Instructor's office at RAF Valley and told him of my wish, which he seemed to receive favourably. I was, however, somewhat concerned when a few days later a notice went up on the squadron noticeboard asking for volunteers for the display pilot slot, but in the end I needn't have worried. Just before Christmas I was told that I had got the job and, a few hours later, I found out that I would be posted back to a frontline Jaguar squadron after the season ended – most definitely a Dry Blackthorn day!

I now had the job of designing my show, and the Christmas holiday in which to do it. Until then, the lowest height I had flown aerobatic manoeuvres at was 5000 ft, so I had no first-hand experience of the aircraft's performance at 500 ft. However, I

BELOW: Diagramatic description of the full show flown by RAF Chivenor's display pilot, Flt Lt Ian Wood

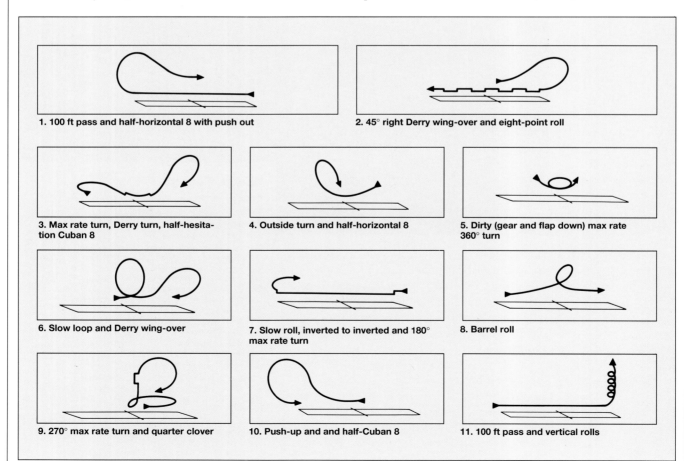

1. 100 ft pass and half-horizontal 8 with push out

2. 45° right Derry wing-over and eight-point roll

3. Max rate turn, Derry turn, half-hesitation Cuban 8

4. Outside turn and half-horizontal 8

5. Dirty (gear and flap down) max rate 360° turn

6. Slow loop and Derry wing-over

7. Slow roll, inverted to inverted and 180° max rate turn

8. Barrel roll

9. 270° max rate turn and quarter clover

10. Push-up and and half-Cuban 8

11. 100 ft pass and vertical rolls

LEFT: In 1993 two Hawk T.1As did the rounds as display aircraft, and both wore all-black colour schemes. This pristine example represented the 'Welsh Air Force' at 29 events both in the UK and Europe, travelling as far afield as Malta and Denmark during the course of the season. Its pilot was Flt Lt Geraint Herbert, a QFI attached to the Standards Flight of No 4 FTS at Valley. This photograph was taken at the Biggin Hill Air Fair moments after rotation on 20 June 1993, Geraint flying his full show on this occasion. The flight provided its pilot with the two most amusing incidents of his season – firstly, Air Traffic Control asked him to adjust the setting on his transponder whilst he was inverted in the middle of his display, and secondly, when he came up the valley on approach to Biggin at the completion of his performance, a London taxi drove across the runway threshold about five seconds before he touched down! *(Photo by Cliff Knox)*

had watched many Hawk displays and had a fair idea of what could be achieved, so I sat down at the table with a pencil and paper and began drawing.

The Hawk is quite an agile aircraft with a performance stretching from +8 to -3.5g, but it is not particularly fast or loud. I decided to position my display as close to the crowd as I could, which meant flying the aircraft at about 30 to 50 kts slower than many previous Hawk displays – using a datum speed of 300 kts would give me a smaller turn radius, plus allow me to use a display line closer to the crowd than at the higher speed. The aircraft would have an impressive initial turn rate at this velocity, and would be able to sustain between +5 and 6g, as well as achieve -3.5g. I felt that it was important to use the negative 'g' available because, although very uncomfortable, it showed a capability which was unusual in jet aircraft.

After many attempts, I arrived at my final 'paper' display. I was pleased with it as far as it went, but had no real idea if the individual manoeuvres would link together well, or if they would stay in the same piece of airspace – an obvious requirement! There was only one thing for it. I would have to get airborne and experiment. The rest of the holiday went by slowly as I waited for my chance.

At the start of 1993 I finally got my hands on a Hawk again and started to practice my sequence with a base height of 5000 ft. My flying for the previous three-and-a-half years had been as a tactics and weapons instructor at RAF Brawdy in west Wales, and aerobatics were not a part of the syllabus. It took me a week of practice before I managed to fly out of loops on the same heading that I had entered them! I also obtained two black eyes due to the effect of so much negative 'g'.

Finally, I established that the display did flow quite nicely, and it was then time to bring it over the airfield to find out if it 'walked'. It was also time to lower the base height. The work-down involved flying six practices at 1500 and 1000 ft before getting to 500 ft, and at each height the margin for error reduced. However, by this stage I was so familiar with my sequence that I could recite it backwards at the end of Happy Hour, and errors were not of safety but more of allowing (or not) for the wind.

I had discovered that my show would stay over the airfield that it had started from, but that the real work was in adjusting for the wind, which had a habit of never being the same twice. Most debriefs were spent discussing how I should cope with different wind witds with my supervisor.

The display season was due to start for me in the middle of May. Before I could display in front of the public, however, I had to be given the authority to do so by the AOC RAF Support Command. All the would-be display pilots had to fly their sequence for his approval, and for various

BELOW: Carrying just enough fuel to perform its display, the Hawk rotates rapidly after brakes off at the runway threshold. With plenty of tarmac still beneath him, 'Woody' has already cycled away the undercarriage and raised the flaps. Unlike the Harrier GR.7 display, which commences virtually the second Rob leaves terra firma, the Hawk pilots would clear show centre and allow the relatively underpowered jet to build up a head of steam prior to initiating the first manoeuvre (Photo by John Dibbs)

reasons, most of them involving the British weather, clearance was delayed until 5 pm on the evening before my first public display! I was very nervous, and the best that could be said about my performance was that it was safe! But I was given my clearance and so packed my bag and set off for the season.

THE MILDENHALL TEST

Amongst my first displays was Mildenhall Air Fete 93, one of the biggest shows in the world, with a crowd line nearly two miles long. On the Sunday of the two-day event the wind was right on the limits for my aircraft, and many participants were forced to pull out. Not only that, the wind was all across the runway and blowing onto the crowd – the worst kind. My display slot had been brought forward, thus eating into my preparation time, so I was a bit rushed. Despite all this, I still managed to get to the holding point with a

few minutes to spare, and I sat there with butterflies in my stomach rehearsing the sequence.

Finally, I lined up on the runway and was cleared to take-off and display. I selected full power, satisfied myself that everything was as it should be, and released the brakes. With a low fuel weight the Hawk accelerates quite briskly and soon I was airborne and raising the undercarriage and flap. At the end of the runway I pulled left through 45° and climbed to check the cloudbase. It was just high enough for my full show so I turned back to the right, hoping that I had allowed enough for the wind, and picked up the display line over my shoulder.

BELOW RIGHT: Like its compatriot at Valley, the Chivenor display Hawk has benefited from the tender love and attention lavished upon it by polish-toting aircraftsmen. Photographed early on in the season, and prior to it receiving the base's distinctive battleaxe motif on its fin, XX230 nevertheless proudly boasts yellow triangles under the wings. Like the Valley Hawk, Chivenor's aircraft was flown by a Standards Flight pilot in the form of Flt Lt Ian Wood, who served with No 7 FTS from 1992 until his posting to Holloman AFB, New Mexico, and the F-117A Stealth Fighter at the end of the 1993 display season. His previous flying experience included a tour on Tornado GR.1s with No IX Sqn and a spell as a QWI on Hawk T.1As with No 63 Sqn at Chivenor (Photo by John Dibbs)

I descended to 100 ft and accelerated to 400 kts for an initial high speed pass, and half way along the runway turned at 8g to the right, pulled up and flew a teardrop back towards the line. This time as I passed the start of the display line, at 350 kts, I rolled the aircraft inverted and started to look for the display datum, where I flew a twinkle roll back into the inverted position and then continued to the other end of the line. I rolled the aircraft through 270° and pulled into a 7.5g turn to the left, allowing the speed to decrease to 300 kts while I strained to look over my shoulder again for datum.

Next came a Derry reversal to head out on a 45° line and then a pull to 75° nose up, rolling inverted and waiting for my 'Gate' of 3600 ft and 200 kts before pulling through and looking up and out of the canopy for datum. A quick check that the speed was not so high that I would exceed the negative g-limit, and I rolled right through 120° and pushed the control column onto the front stop. The seat straps flew up into my face as I pushed around the corner at -3.5g, following a

heading that took me out on the 45° line away from datum again. I rolled to inverted and held it into wind for a short while before flying a hesitation roll to briefly regain erect flight.

A quick pause for breath before straining and pulling up again, this time for a half-horizontal 8 to finish 60° nose down, pointing back towards the runway. At 1500 ft I snapped the aircraft level

BELOW: The man and his machine take a break during the pre-season work-ups. Geraint wears a No 74(R) Sqn patch on his right sleeve, the 'Tigers' serving alongside No 234(R) Sqn within No 4 FTS. Although initially part of the former unit, Geraint was soon chosen to join the hand-picked team of QFIs who constitute the Standards Flight, their task being to teach the instructors within the Valley FTS the art of advanced tactical flying. Geraint had completed a tour with No 54 Sqn on Jaguar GR.1s at RAF Coltishall before joining the Hawk community at RAF Brawdy, where he was trained as a QWI. Having left Valley at the end of 1993, he is now back flying Jaguars, this time with No 41 Sqn

and immediately pulled onto the line and rolled inverted. I looked up for the end of the line and then rolled into a 270° turn, pausing after each 90°. Following completion of the final roll, I looked to ensure I was in the right place, pulled hard into the vertical, rolled 90° towards the line and pulled over the top, checking for the gate, before pointing vertically down at the datum and recovering to 500 ft, running out on the 45° line.

This whole series of manoeuvres was very difficult to adjust accurately for wind, but this time it worked well and I grunted a sigh of relief while pulling back towards the runway for the slow roll. At the far end I chopped the throttle and turned hard back towards datum, while slowing down to 200 kts so that I could drop the gear and flaps. I flew a level 360° turn, adjusting the 'g' while pointing into wind so that I could use the allowable 2.5g on the way back towards the line. With about 60° of the turn left I raised the gear and flap and, with 200 kts on the clock, pulled up into a loop. During this manoeuvre I had to ensure I didn't waste any energy by entering the pre-stall buffet, so I needed to be very smooth on the controls.

As I passed the vertical I rolled through a few degrees into wind so that I didn't get blown over the line (the worst crime a display pilot can commit) and looked for my gate of 3100 ft. Upside down, I scanned the ground for the runway and saw that I was still on the display side of the line, so I was able to complete the manoeuvre, pulling through and recovering to 500 ft. A maximum rate turn through 180° away from the crowd displaced me enough to allow me to perform a barrel roll back onto the line. This manoeuvre is a continuous roll and pull with no specific gates, and as such can be difficult to judge. Most pilots who include it in their sequence are especially careful while flying it, and I was no exception.

As soon as I was back at 500 ft and on the line again, I pulled up for another half-horizontal eight. I rolled in the vertical to adjust for the wind again, and pulled to 60° nose down. At 2900 ft I pushed the control against the front stop and pushed out, looking over the nose for the horizon to appear so that I could co-ordinate the level off at 500 ft and run out inverted. I re-positioned for the break to land and then taxied in just ten minutes after getting airborne. As I opened the canopy to get out, still panting, I was asked what the vast crowd had looked like from the air. I answered 'What crowd?!'

Displaying the Hawk professionally proved to be the most demanding flying I have ever done and, therefore, the most rewarding. It was well into the season before I was working at a level where I could snatch the odd second to glance out at the crowd and actually enjoy myself. Interestingly enough, it was also at about that time that I started to receive some positive comments about my show.

There were many highlights and incidents as I travelled about which ranged from Air Traffic Control asking me to adjust the setting on my transponder while I was upside down, to a London Taxi driving across the runway about five seconds before I was going to land!. I was told at the beginning by a seasoned display pilot that I should expect two displays to be disasters, two to be fantastic and the rest to be just run of the mill. I must have had a good season because I had my two disasters, but I also flew three shows that made everything worthwhile.

And now, of course, I never want to go to another airshow in my life!

RIGHT: Geoff Lee flew with No 7 FTS once the jet had received its full display scheme. He has logged hundreds of hours on fast jets recording on film the finest British Aerospace products available, and one of his favourite angles places his subject in the vertical, diving towards the camera. By positioning XX230 at such an attitude, Geoff has been able to feature all the marking details applied by the No 7 FTS paint shop in a single photograph (Photo by Geoff Lee/ British Aerospace via Mike Stroud)

BELOW: Flt Lt Herbert's full show as flown in 1993

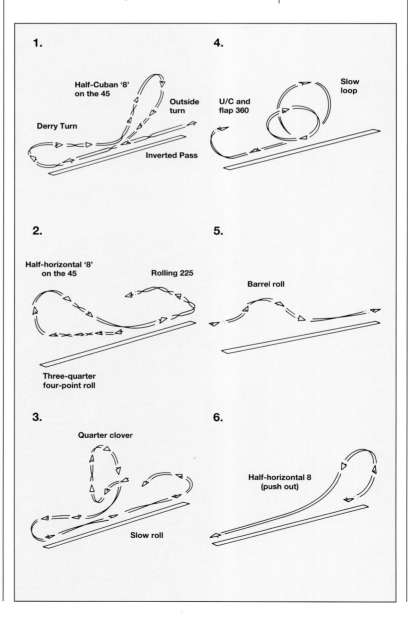

Individual show reports as officially filed by Flt Lt Herbert

VENUE	DATE	DISPLAY

FAF Cognac   Sat 15 May   Rolling

PDA granted for Rolling display at 1700 on the Friday so departure to Cognac delayed until Saturday, which required Valley to open specially. Rolling display flown in perfect weather. Display parallel to runway with well marked display line. Well organised display but accommodation barely adequate.

FAF Istres   Sun 16 May   Rolling

Well organised display with good accommodation. Rolling display in fantastic weather.

RAF   Sat/Sun   Full
Mildenhall   29/30 May

Two full displays, the second with 25 kts on-crowd wind. Excellent accommodation. The biggest moan was the 40 minutes to an hour wait every time we asked for fuel; my aircraft was on the display side of the airfield and it took two-and-a-half-hours to get there, fly the ten-minute display, refuel and return to the crowd side!

RAF Odiham   Fri 4 June   Full

Well organised display with good hosting and domestic arrangements.

RDAF Aalborg   Sun 6 Jun   Full

Display datum was not marked on the airfield and was poorly located at the end of the crowd line. The same frequency was used for Ground, Tower and Display, and there was continual chatter throughout my display. The accommodation was poor, with only a sofa-bed to sleep on, and the meals provided were not acceptable. The show was the first in Denmark since 1988 and this showed in the organisation.

RAF Coningsby   Sat 12 Jun   Rolling

The first display that applied pressure to minimise the numbers of support crew. Good accommodation in local hotels. First available transport to hotels was 2100 on the Friday, which was a bit late. Well organised display, but the weather was so poor that it forced me fly a Rolling rather than Full show.

RAF Locking   Sat 19 Jun   Full

My first display at a non-airfield site. Well organised except that I lost the Halton show because both venues could not agree mutually acceptable slot times that would allow me perform near consecutive routines. Display frequency was unreadable until I was almost overhead the site, and then it was almost continually used as a do-it-yourself Air Traffic Control service by two helicopter pilots operating nearby.

Biggin Hill   Sat 20 Jun   Full

Generally a well run show with excellent accommodation and domestic arrangements. The display frequency, however, was being used by at least two other ATC agencies. I was asked to squawk while upside down in my second manoeuvre, and just as I was about to land a London taxi drove across the runway slightly short of the threshold!

Woodford   Sat 26 Jun   Flat

Very well organised show. Poor weather on the day caused many changes to the published schedule. I spent 30 minutes holding IMC prior to my show. Then, because the *Flanker* decided to give an impromptu performance, I was asked to divert to Valley! After a few comments from me I was allowed in to fly my flat show.

RAF Swanton   Sun 27 Jun   Full
Morley

Another well organised show on the operational side. I flew a Full display and then landed at Norwich, who provided a very good service.

RAF   Fri/Sat 2/3 Jul   Both Full
Waddington

A well organised display. Good accommodation.

Ramsey   Tues 6 Jul   Full

A last minute request for a display off Ramsey, Isle of Man, for the closure of RAF Jurby. It was my first performance over the sea, but excellent weather and horizon posed few problems and I flew my Full display.

Newtownards   Sat 10 Jul   Full

A break in the weather allowed me to fly my Full show. No other comments apart from the fact that this was yet another site where there was only one frequency available.

RAF Buchan   Sat 17 Jul   DNCO

The weather at Buchan was unfit to even fly through the site so I had to return to Leuchars. The only display I had to cancel due to weather.

Bruntingthorpe Sat 18 Jul   Full

A well organised and friendly display from the domestic point of view. The briefed display datum, however, was at the end of the crowd line.

RAF   Sun 18 Jul   Full
Church Fenton

My only comment on this performance is that I found the display line and datum difficult to see from the air.

RAF Odiham   Tues 27 Jul   Rolling

At this event, the display aircraft were part of the static park before the show started, the barriers being opened and closed in accordance with aircraft arrivals. At the start of the actual display, the Tornado and Harriers were forced to start and taxy through a pan full of people.

RAF Shawbury Thurs 29 Jul   Full

Timing was a problem during this show. ATC did not seem to be abreast of a changing situation and I was finally left with a race to the holding point to make a new slot time, which then slipped again and resulted in me having to wait at the threshold.

RAF Leeming Sat 31 Jul   Full

Full display in a tricky wind. No other comments.

RAF Valley   Sat 31 Jul   Full

The best timing of any display during the season. Well organised.

RAE Aberporth Wed 18 Aug   Full

No comment.

Carlisle   Sat/Sun 28/29 Aug   Both
Rolling

A friendly, well run show. It was another example, however, of a small airfield site using only one frequency for ground and display use.

NAB Schleswig Sat 4 Sep   Flat

The German authorities would not allow any 'over the top' manoeuvres and, consequently, my Full and Rolling displays were both rejected. The constraints were made for the sake of safety, but meant that I was performing the display that I use the least. My departure time for Belgium was dictated by model aircraft flying, which could not be stopped for me to take-off – very frustrating.

Zoersal   Sat/Sun 4/5 Sep   Both Full
Oostmalle
Outstanding.

Duxford   Sun 12 Sep   Full
Excellent accommodation. Well run operationally.

Southport   Sun 12 Sep   Full
Well run in all aspects.

ABOVE: The end result of Geoff Lee's air-to-air sortie was a stunning sequence of shots all bearing his distinctive trademarks of pin sharp clarity and full frame action. Pulling in behind the photographer's Hawk cameraship, 'Woody' has held formation until breaking left on Geoff's command. This angle best highlights the gold chevron motif applied in glossy lacquer to the jet's polished underside *(Photo by Geoff Lee/British Aerospace via Mike Stroud)*

RAF Leuchars   Sat 18 Sep   Full
I was asked to cut short my display because a Hercules was late getting airborne, which was very frustrating. Otherwise, no comment.

Malta   Sat/Sun 25/26 Sep   Full
A first attempt at running an international airshow and there were many small points which the organisers were keen to learn from during the weekend. The main problem, however, concerned the operational aspects of the show, which lacked much of the required detail. It was largely left to the display crews to ensure the flying ran smoothly, and this was possible because there were only four displays. This was a very friendly show and I believe that many of the problems encountered this time will be solved by next year.

RAF Cranwell   Tues 28 Sep   Roll
No comment.   □

British Aerospace Hawk T.1

Country of Origin: United Kingdom

Type: Two-seat multi-purpose trainer and light tactical aircraft

Powerplant: One 5340 lb (2422 kg) Rolls-Royce Turbomeca RT.172-06-11 Adour 151 turbofan

Performance: Max speed, 617 mph (993 km/h) at sea level, 570 mph (917 km/h) at 30,000 ft (9144 m); range cruise, 405 mph (652 km/h) at 30,000 ft (9144 m); time to 40,000 ft (12,192 m), 10 min; service ceiling, 44,000 ft (13,410 m)

Weights: Empty, 7450 lb (3379 kg); normal take-off (trainer), 10,250 lb (4649 kg), (weapons trainer), 12,000 lb (5443 kg); max. take-off, 16,500 lb (7484 kg)

Armament: (Weapons trainer) One hard point on fuselage centreline and two wing hard points and (ground attack) two additional wing hard points, all stressed for loads up to 1000 lb (454 kg). Max external load of 5000 lb (2268 kg)

Status: Single pre-production example flown on 21 August 1974, and first and second production examples flown on 19 May and 22 April 1975, respectively. Total of 175 built for RAF, with first delivery taking place during 1976

Dimensions: Span, 30 ft 10 in (9.40 m); length (including probe), 39 ft 2^1/$_2$ in (11.96 m); height, 13 ft 5 in (4.10 m); wing area, 180 sq ft (16.70 m^2)

Hercules C.1P No 57(R) Squadron

Sqn Ldr Don MacIntosh – Pilot   **Flt Lt Nigel Watson – Pilot**

'THE Herc is a very neat aircraft to fly, and many people are surprised just how tight we can keep the display', commented Flt Lt Nigel Watson, one of two Hercules display captains charged with demonstrating the aircraft's awesome capabilities throughout the 1993 airshow season.

'To me its an excellent display machine. We can pull around 2g, which enables us to keep our routine close to the crowd, showing lots of plan view and keeping the spectator right in on the action. The only thing we lack is a large amount of noise, and flames shooting out of the back, although we do get a cup of coffee whilst airborne – difficult for a fast jet pilot!'

Nigel Watson has over 7000 hours on the Hercules, having flown the type since the early 1970s. As well asserving with several frontline squadrons his career includes tours with the Special Forces and Support and Development Unit. Currently he serves with No 57(R) Sqn (formerly No 242 OCU), the Hercules Operational Conversion Unit. His fellow captain is Sqn Ldr Don MacIntosh, another vastly experienced pilot who can also boast well over 7000 hours on the Lockheed turboprop. He served with No 47 Sqn and the Special Forces prior to joining the Joint Air Transport Establishment (JATE), where he undertook development work flying Air Drop Trials. He currently serves with STANEVAL, which is a unit within the Lyneham transport wing which grades Hercules Instructors.

Both Nigel and Don were involved in *Operation Corporate* – the retaking of the Falkland Islands – flying in some of the famed 24-hour missions, and again both men also served time in the Gulf during *Operation Granby*. More recently, Sqn Ldr MacIntosh was tasked with flying in support of the relief effort in Somalia.

1993 was Don's third year as a display captain, following two seasons in the co-pilot's seat; it was Nigel's second year. In order to minimise the disruption to the display season caused by normal operational taskings, the two captains shared the workload, drawing the remainder of their crew from a 'pool' of volunteer officers and NCOs.

The main thrust of the display is aimed at demonstrating the Hercules' tactical capabilities, and this involves some very impressive manoeuvres for such a large aircraft. The sequence includes a short field landing and the tactical off-load of either two Land Rovers or two Scorpion light tanks, whilst the Hercules sits poised for a quick get away once they have exited the aircraft. This lively item takes place at the mid-point of the show, and in order for it take place the aircraft carries a larger than average crew, which is comprised of four 'Front-Enders', a load-master and an eight-man off-load team, as well as the drivers and crew of the vehicles.

The routine is usually flown in a standard Hercules C.1P, although it could be performed equally as well in a stretched C.3P. For each display the aircraft is selected 'on the day' from the available airframes at Lyneham. In order to maintain currency the crew must fly the full airshow sequence at least once every six days, with extra sorties being flown if there is a large gap between events. Much of what is practised during normal flying has been included in the Hercules display, thus giving the public a good insight into the aircraft's operational capabilities.

Elements such as the short-field landing, which gives the aircraft the ability to operate from unprepared strips, the low-level flypast, utilised in Ultra Low Level Airdrop (ULLA) operations, and the famous 'Khe Sanh' landing, a method developed by the USAF in Vietnam which enabled the large aircraft to enter an airfield avoiding small arms fire, are all included.

During normal practice sessions both Don and Nigel fly a display trip each, taking it in turns to fill the captain's right-hand seat. The front end crew during the following currency flight performed from Lyneham in mid-July 1993 consisted of Flt Lt Ian Mackay (air engineer), Flt Lt Stu Avent (navigator) and Sgt Neil Franks (load-master), and his off-load team in the back.

RIGHT: Although somewhat slower and far less noisy than most other RAF 'performers' that regularly feature at airshows across the UK, the Hercules C.1P is, however, renowned for its incredible agility and breathtaking tactical take-offs and landings. Always displayed with a vigour and professionalism that roots the crowd to the spot in sheer disbelief, the Hercules routine in 1993 was ably performed by a crew who between them had over 14,000 hours on type! Typically, two pilots are selected by the Lyneham Wing to fly the entire season, the pilots performing alternate displays in the right-hand seat of the Hercules. The captains for 1993 were Flt Lt Nigel Watson, an instructor with No 57(R) Sqn, and Sqn Ldr Don MacIntosh of the Standards Evaluation (STANEVAL) flight, who spends his weekdays grading Hercules instructors. The displays are flown in a 'stock' C.1P selected at Lyneham usually on the day of the airshow itself, and for the Mildenhall Air Fete weekend in late May XV186 performed the honours. To ensure a spectacular departure, the crew bump the rotation speed up from 80 to 115 kts at the start of their routine, using some 2500 ft of runway in the process. With the gear and flaps still cycling, the aircraft is reefed into a left hand climbing turn away from the crowd-line, the pilot levelling off at 1000 ft *(Photo by Tony Holmes)*

LEFT: The tactical landing and vehicle disembarkation is one of the most popular routines performed at any airshow. For several years the Hercules would disgorge a clutch of Scorpion light tanks, which would roar around the airfield like radio-controlled cars. However, due no doubt to ever-shrinking budgets, the Lyneham Wing was forced in 1993 to substitute their hyperactive armoured vehicles with 'soft top' Land Rovers equipped with general purpose machine guns and psychedelic smoke canisters. It is the job of the eight-man Mobile Air Movements team to ensure that the pair of Landrovers, and their passengers, are off-loaded both rapidly and safely – the time from touchdown to take-off should not exceed 75 seconds *(Photo by Tony Holmes)*

In the right-hand seat, Don MacIntosh takes the first run, Nigel Watson strapping in to the co-pilot's seat. With the four Allison T56 turboprops fully wound up and all the pre-flight checks completed, the aircraft is cleared onto Lyneham's main runway. Don obtains his clearance from the tower, the engines are run up to take-off power, and following a check all round, the brakes are released and the display is on.

'I have control' announces the captain as the aircraft hurtles down the runway. Tactical rotation speed for the Hercules is around 80 kts, but in order to maintain a steeper climb out, the display speed is set at 115 kts. As soon as this point is reached, following a take-off run of 2500 ft, Don pulls back on the stick and the aircraft leaps off the tarmac. Almost immediately, the Hercules is heaved into a left-hand climbing turn, banking across the airfield and levelling out at 1000 ft. From this altitude the pilot pre-positions himself for a 'run and break' along the display line.

The aircraft's vast cockpit glazing allows an excellent view forward as it is lined up on the runway centreline from about a mile out.

A steep descent levels the Hercules at 100 ft, and the speed is increased to 210 kts as the threshold is reached. After powering down the runway, the aircraft is again banked into a climbing turn, which levels at 300 ft, before reversing course for another sharp descent into the short field landing. As the aircraft breaks into the turn Don calls 'Flaps and gear down'.

'Gear down', is the immediate reply.

'All greens', calls Nigel Watson, confirming that the undercarriage has indeed cycled down and locked into position.

'One minute', replies Don, announcing to Neil Franks and the off-load team in the back how long it will be before they will be stationary on the ground. This gives them the opportunity to start their engines and prepare for exit. The Hercules flares and touches down on the runway.

'Red-On' calls the pilot, as he slams the engines into reverse.

The 'Red-On' call is the signal to the load master to lower the ramp and begin unfastening the restraining chains on the vehicles. In a plume of spray thrown up from the wet tarmac, the aircraft comes to a standstill at its designated mid-runway point. 'Green-On' is the call, and the vehicles deploy.

'Ramp coming up' calls Neil Franks, at which point Don reverses the Hercules 100 ft down the runway, slewing the aircraft at a 45° angle across the tarmac as the vehicles cross in front of it and speed away trailing smoke from orange flares.

'Ten seconds to ramp lock', calls Neil Franks over the intercom.

Don counts down the seconds and as the ramp locks up, once again full power is applied and the aircraft surges forward. As the Hercules is already half way down the tarmac the end of the runway quickly comes into view, and with rotation speed reached a sharp pull on the control column sends it into a 30° climb. The gear and flaps stay down and at the top of the climb Don once more calls for 'Ramp down'.

The aircraft now breaks at 700 ft, winging over into a 125-kt descent and pulling out at 200 ft, with power on to give the spectator an excellent view inside the rear of the Hercules as it climbs away. Levelling off at 500 ft, Don pulls a hard turn and descends, stabilising height at a mere 15 ft off the deck as again they hurtle down the runway for the Ultra Low Level Flypast. Pitching up at the end into a 360° turn away from

BELOW RIGHT: Nigel Watson's season started in ideal fashion when he, and his crew, were awarded the highly coveted John Watt Memorial Trophy for performing the best display at the 1993 Fighter Meet at North Weald, which was held on 15/16 May. Pitted against a host of other types ranging from a Fokker Dr.1 Triplane replica, through Spitfires and Mustangs to modern RAF 'heavy metal', the Hercules crew impressed the judges with a slick seven-minute display that included low level runs, vehicle offloading, a 'Khe Sanh', or Sarajevo, approach and short field landing. This award was a first for the Lyneham Wing, and Nigel Watson (centre) was presented with the trophy by the station Commander, Gp Capt David Adams – the other key crewmembers were, from left to right, Flt Lt Simon Thompson (pilot), Flt Lt Stu Avent (navigator) and Sgt Andy Seddon (airloadmaster). Flight engineer for the display, Sgt 'Bones' Brown, is missing from the line up (Photo via Nigel Watson)

ABOVE: Once aligned with crowd centre, the pilot pushes the control column forward and steeply descends to 100 ft, building up his speed throughout the dive until he reaches 215 knots. Powering down the runway, he again pulls into a tight left hand climbing turn just past the proposed off-loading point for his next tactical demonstration. Banking over the tank farm at Mildenhall, Flt Lt Watson scans the runway ahead of him whilst simultaneously feeding on the power and keeping a watchful eye on his altimeter. His kneepads, which contain his notes, are visible through the cockpit transparency, as is the head of one of the off-load team members positioned in the astrodome *(Photo by Tony Holmes)*

the crowdline, he calls for 'Gear and flaps up' and 'Ramp up', putting the aircraft once again into clean configuration once again.

Climbing away, Don breaks into a tight wingover, gathering speed to 200 kts as the aircraft makes a further pass at 200 ft, climbing steeply away at its conclusion. The pilot once again calls for 'Gear and flaps' as the Hercules steadies at 1000 ft, lined up on the runway centreline half a mile out for the final sequence.

The spectacular finale is the 'Khe Sanh' landing, one of the most impressive sequences performed by any aircraft. Nearing the end of the runway the aircraft is pitched nose down into the near vertical, the threshold 'piano keys' rushing up to meet it – the sensation is further heightened by the negative 'g' of the pitch-over.

As the Hercules goes through a pre-determined 'gate height', Don eases the stick back and the aircraft glides onto the runway, accompanied by a squeak of rubber and the throttling back of the T56s. 'Seven-and-a-half minutes. Not bad', comments a satisfied Nigel Watson.

Lockheed Hercules C.1P

Country of Origin: USA

Type: Medium- to long-range military transport
Powerplant: Four 4050 eshp Allison T56-A-7A turboprops

Performance: Max speed, 384 mph (618 km/h); max cruise, 368 mph (592 km/h); econ cruise, 340 mph (547 km/h); range (with max payload and five per cent plus 30 min reserves), 2450 miles (3943 km); max range, 4770 miles (7657 km); initial climb, 1900 ft/min (9.64 m/sec)

Weights: Empty equipped, 72,892 lb (33,063 kg); max normal take-off, 155,000 lb (70,301 kg); max overload, 175,000 lb (79,380 kg)

Accommodation: Flight crew of four and max of 92 fully-equipped troops, 64 paratroops, or 74 casualty stretchers and two medical attendants. As a cargo carrier, up to six pre-loaded freight pallets may be carried

Status: The C-130H is the principal current version of the Hercules which, in progressively developed forms, has been in continuous production since 1952. RAF early customer for the Hercules, and still operators of the largest fleet of aircraft outside of the USAF – 66 airframes delivered from 1967

Dimensions: Span, 132 ft 7 in (40.41 m); length 97 ft 9 in (29.78 m); height 38 ft 3 in (11.66 m); wing area 1745 sq ft (162.12m^2)

Nimrod MR.Mk2P No 42(R) Squadron

Sqn Ldr Roy Bouch – Pilot   Flt Lt Keith Harding – Co-Pilot
Flt Lt Tony Graves – Air Engineer

THE Nimrod MR.Mk2P is a long range maritime patrol aircraft with roles of anti-submarine warfare, anti-surface unit warfare and search and rescue. Despite budgetary constraints and the need to fly operational missions at home and overseas, the RAF does its best to ensure that Nimrod aircraft are available to display at most of the major venues, subject to an invitation from airshow organisers. During 1993, Nimrod aircraft displayed at

December 1990. He currently serves as the NOCU Chief Flying Instructor.

Sitting in the left-hand seat alongside Sqn Ldr Bouch is Flt Lt Keith Harding, the NOCU display co-pilot. Since joining the RAF in February 1984 he has spent virtually his entire career on Nimrods, only 200 hours of the 2600 total in his log book

25 UK and 4 North American air shows.

Sqn Ldr Roy Bouch is the display pilot for the Nimrod Operational Conversion Unit (NOCU), otherwise known as No 42(Reserve) Squadron, based at RAF Kinloss. He joined the RAF in November 1976 and has a total of 4500 flying hours, 2800 of which are on the Nimrod. After tours as a Nimrod pilot on No 120 Sqn from September 1979 to September 1984, Roy spent the next four years flying Jet Provosts as a Qualified Flying Instructor, before assuming the command of the University of Glasgow and Strathclyde Air Squadron from August 1988 to

having been spent on other types. After flying a long five-year tour as a Nimrod pilot on No 206 Sqn between January 1987 and March 1992, Keith was posted to the NOCU as an instructor.

The third full-time member of the crew is Flt Lt Tony Graves, who joined the RAF way back in April 1970 as a radar technician, before entering the ranks of the airman aircrew. Over the years he has amassed over 3100 hours in his logbook as an air engineer, flying initially with No 201 Sqn from March 1981 to September 1984. He was then posted to Finningley as an Air Engineer Instructor, staying in South

Yorkshire until October 1987. Achieving the rank of Engineer Leader upon returning to No 120 Sqn in November 1988, he stayed with the unit until October 1991, when he was posted to the NOCU as Chief Air Engineer Instructor.

No 42(R) Sqn learnt that it was providing a display crew for the 1993 season in February of that year. Becoming a member of the team involved a process of being nominated by the Officer Commanding RAF Kinloss, Grp Capt Neal, followed by the approval of his suggestion by AOC No 18 Group, Air Marshal Sir John Harris. Nomination was based on experience and ability to fill the role. The selected crew flew a standard routine laid down and formatted in No 18 Group Air Staff Orders, which contrasted with their fast jet brethren who could vary their displays from year to year depending on the inventiveness of the pilot.

The Nimrod is a large aircraft, with a wingspan of 115 ft and a length of 130 ft, and the main aim of the display is to demonstrate how manoeuvrable it is for its size. This is typical of

the type of per-
formance required to
turn and attack a submarine in the
minimum time. With these parameters in mind, the team began work-ups by performing a dedicated display practice sortie on 30 April 1993.

'For the first run we used minimum operating heights of 500 ft for turns and 300 ft for straight and level passes. Subsequent display runs during and after that sortie were conducted to our laid down minima of 300 ft for turns and 100 ft for straight and level passes', explained Keith Harding.

Three more practice sorties were flown, with

two full displays being performed per flight, on 4, 5 and 6 May 1993 respectively, resulting in approval from the AOC on the afternoon following the final rehearsal.

THE DISPLAY

Keith Harding gave the following detailed description of the full routine, as flown at a typical airshow venue in normal weather conditions: 'We aim to be at a suitable holding point, which is usually five to ten nautical miles (nm) on the extended centre line of the display axis, at about 15 minutes prior to our agreed display slot time. This is to allow for any changes to the airshow programme.

'Once ATC have cleared us to begin the display, we run from crowd left at a height of 300 ft and a speed of 220 kts. At one nautical mile from the display datum the landing and taxy lights go on. On reaching the display datum

the airbrakes are selected out and a steep turn to the left is started, climbing to 500 ft and using up to 60° angle of bank, dependant upon wind conditions. When the speed has reduced to 190 kts, the airbrakes are selected in.

Caught moments after raising the gear at the beginning of the crew's very first public display, flown at the 1993 Mildenhall Air Fete, the Nimrod's four Rolls-Royce Spey Mk 250 turbojets belch out a trail of smoke denoting that Sqn Ldr Bouch has the throttles pushed forward to the stops in an effort to reach his prescribed manoeuvring height. A physically impressive aircraft that boasts a wingspan and length that both easily surpass 110 ft, the Nimrod's 'presence' at an airshow is further emphasized by the ear-splitting note of its four Speys, which share a remarkably similar engine note with the quartet of Bristol Olympus turbojets that powered the late lamented Vulcan! Indeed, many airshow goers now look to the 'Mighty Hunter' to fill the gap left by the grounded Avro delta (Photo by Tony Holmes)

RIGHT: The 1993 display crew hailed from the Nimrod Operational Conversion Unit (NOCU), or No 42(R) Sqn as they were rebadged in early 1993, and consisted of pilot, Sqn Ldr Roy Bouch (centre), co-pilot, Flt Lt Keith Harding (left) and air engineer, Flt Lt Tony Graves (right) – a clutch of supporting engineers and assorted aircrew from Kinloss would help make up the numbers, particularly during deployments some distance away from Scotland. All veterans with several frontline tours to their credit, this highly experienced trio performed at 25 airshows in the UK and four in North America during the course of 1993 (Photo by RAF Kinloss Photographic Section)

As the turn is continued the aircraft approaches the crowd once more, the bomb doors are selected open and the searchlight switched on as the aircraft descends to pass the datum at 300 ft and 190 kts. The climbing and descending turns during the orbits give the show spectator the impression that the aircraft is flying level.

'Whilst we pull away from the crowd for another port orbit, the bomb doors are closed and the searchlight is selected off. Flaps are progressively lowered to 40° to reduce the speed to 160 kts. As the speed reduces through 185 kts the landing gear is selected down and the aircraft descends to 300 ft to pass the datum for a 'dirty' fly-by using 45° angle of bank.

'Abeam the datum full power is applied momentarily again, the aircraft turning right 70° away from the display line and climbing to 1000 ft in a steep dumb-bell to the right. During this manoeuvre the pilot is unable to maintain visual contact with the display axis and datum, so the co-pilot guides him onto the display line.

'Crew co-operation is very important throughout the display sequence as visibility from the cockpit is extremely poor with large angles of bank. The right turn continues, the power is reduced and flap is selected to 60° as the speed reduces through 150 kts. The Nimrod descends to line up with and fly down the display line at a height of 100 ft in the landing configuration, this low speed manoeuvre being flown at 130 kts.

'Abeam the datum full power is again applied momentarily, the aircraft turning right 70° away from the display line and climbing to 1000 ft in a steep dumb-bell to the left as the flaps are selected to 20° and the landing gear is selected up. The left turn continues and the aircraft descends. When lined up with the display axis, flap is selected up and the speed is allowed to increase to 230 kts for a 'clean' flypast from the crowd left to right at 100 ft.

'Now abeam the datum once again, but this time at 230 kts, full power is applied, with a pitch up to 40° attitude for a steep climb, followed by a wingover to the left as the speed passes through 190 kts. Positive 'g' is applied at all times during this manoeuvre. If conditions permit, before the wingover is started a single or double headed flare is fired by the air engineer from his Very pistol, mounted in the cockpit roof.

'At the end of this final manoeuvre the aircraft will be at 3500 ft, and the radio call of 'display complete' is made to ATC.'

The display is always performed with the crowd to the aircraft's right, so if the runway in use requires the crew to take-off with the crowd on the left, then at a height not below 300 ft a right turn is made away from the centre line, enabling the jet to position for a run in from crowd left.

BELOW: Lights ablaze and bomb bay doors ajar, the Nimrod cruises past the crowd at Mildenhall at 300 ft and 190 kts, with a 60° angle of bank. This part of the routine graphically illustrates the aircraft's impressive agility and low speed/height performance, attributes which are called in to play when the crew are prosecuting a sub-surface contact out over the Atlantic or North Sea during everyday operations *(Photo by Tony Holmes)*

For the crew to maintain currency they have to fly at least one practice routine, which may be an actual public display, at sometime during the eight days leading up to a scheduled airshow performance. In any event, they have to fly at least one supervised display every 30 days.

The highlight of the crew's 1993 display season was participating in the Abbotsford International Airshow, held in British Columbia between 6 and 8 August. Due to it falling on an 'odd' year, the event also incorporated 'Air Show Canada', North America's biggest aerospace trade show. The Nimrod was displayed every day to crowds which eventually totalled nearly 420,000.

In order to emphasise the multi-national flavour of the event, and particularly the presence of the Russian Knights aerobatic team – their visit to Abbotsford was their only sojourn to a Western airshow for 1993 – the NOCU crew had the great honour and privilege of closing the airshow when they participated in a fly-by in close formation with a Russian Knight's Su-27, a US Navy T-45 and a Canadian CF-18 aircraft. The No 42(R) Sqn contingent were also awarded the trophy for 'Best Social Contributors to Air Show 93', although how they qualified for this prize remains a mystery. . . !

Hawker Siddeley Nimrod MR.Mk 2P

Country of Origin: United Kingdom

Type: Long-range maritime patrol aircraft

Powerplant: Four 1160 lb (5515 kg) Rolls-Royce RB.168-20 Spey Mk 250 turbofans

Performance: Max speed, 575 mph (926 km/h); max transit speed, 547 mph (880 km/h); econ transit speed, 490 mph (787 km/h); typical ferry range, 5180-5755 miles (8340-9265 km); typical endurance, 12 hrs

Weights: Max take-off, 177,500 lb (80,510 kg); max overload, 192,000 lb (87,090 kg)

Armament: Ventral weapons bay accommodating full range of ASW weapons (homing torpedoes, mines, depth charges, etc) plus two underwing pylons on each side for total of two Harpoon ASMs, or AIM-9 Sidewinders for self-protection

Accommodation: Normal operating crew of 12 with two pilots and flight engineeer on flight deck and nine navigators and sensor operators in tacitcal compartment

Status: First of two Nimrod prototypes employing modified Comet 4C airframes flown 23 May 1967. First of initial batch of 38 production Nimrod MR.Mk 1s flown on 28 June 1968. Completion of this batch in August 1972, followed by delivery of three Nimrod R.Mk 1s for special electronics reconnaissance, and eight more MR.Mk1s built in 1976. All aircraft modified to MR.Mk2P standard in the mid-1980s

Dimensions: Span, 114 ft 10 in (35.00 m); length, 126 ft 9 in (38.63 m); height 29 ft 8½ in (9.01 m); wing area, 2121 sq ft (197.05 m²)

Buccaneer S.2B No 208 Squadron

Flt Lt Neil Benson – Pilot   **Flt Lt Gary Davies – Navigator**

FIRST learned to fly as a raw 18-year-old after joining the UAS whilst reading geography at the University of Strathclyde. Following my graduation in 1983, I joined the RAF and, after Officer Training, completed Basic Flying Training on the Jet Provost at Cranwell. A posting to Advanced Flying Training at RAF Valley on the Hawk ensued, and then I was 'creamed off' and returned to the Jet Provost, learning to become a QFI at RAF Scampton before being posted to Cranwell (again!) as an instructor.

After serving my time as a QFI, I was eventually sent back to Hawks at Valley for a brief 'refresher', then to RAF Brawdy for tactical weapons training. After what seemed like an eternity within the Training Command structure, I finally got my hands on a frontline jet in the form of the Buccaneer S.2B upon graduation from the TWU, my new posting seeing me attached to No 237 OCU at RAF Lossiemouth in early 1990. Having learnt to fly and fight the jet, a posting to No 208 Sqn followed, where I remained until the demise of the Buccaneer in March 1994. I am currently back on the Hawk at Valley, but this time in an instructional role. However, let us return to 1993 and the Buccaneer.

If I sit back and think what an airshow crowd most wants to see in a display – technically impressive aerobatic manoeuvres, or low, fast, thunderous passes – then I'd have to go for the latter. This is just as well really as the 'banana jet', at a display weight of almost 30 tons, was not exactly the most delicate of aerobatic aircraft, and indeed was only cleared for a handful of manoeuvres. Severe limitations which included sustained negative 'g' and no looping manoeuvres

ABOVE: The Buccaneer has been a favourite amongst airshow enthusiasts since the days when Blackburn built aircraft. Literally dozens of Fleet Air Arm and Royal Air Force crews have enjoyed displaying the robust two-seater in front of millions across the UK and western Europe. The distinction of being the final Buccaneer display crew endorsed by the AOC to put the jet through its paces in its last year of service fell to these two gentlemen, Flt Lts Neil Benson (pilot) and Gary Davies (navigator). The Buccaneer S.2B that serves as an impressive backdrop for this 'team' shot has had its roundel zapped by the crew of a visiting Canadian aircraft (Photo via Neil Benson)

reduced the scope even further. What the jet did have going for it though was size, speed and some unique features with which to maintain the public's interest throughout the course of a relatively short routine.

Our display arrival was designed to capture the attention of the crowd – as low as possible-

within the rules (a hard deck of 100 ft) at 570-580 kts (to produce that characteristic 'blue-note' from the twin Speys) and with a touch of bank towards the crowd, which made the jet appear even lower.

The only trouble with this manoeuvre was that some airframes flew sideways at that speed and, to make matters worse, when full aileron was applied at crowd centre, the huge ailerons produced so much adverse aileron yaw that the whole thing was pretty uncomfortable.

A bit of contrast came next, with a 5.5g pull that led into a Derry turn, after which I descended and turned back onto the crowd line and threw everything down – airbrake, flap, aileron droop, tailplane flap, undercarriage and arrester hook – for a 100 ft pass at maximum angle-of-attack/165 kts with a snappy roll (full size nine boot on the rudder to help) at crowd centre. Pulling in the airbrake and applying full power, I could achieve a 40° nose up climb.

Cleaning up involved a bit of left-handed flying as I had to move the autostabs and the aileron gearing to 'high speed', thus reducing the latter's area of travel. Forget this bit amongst the flap, gear and hook movement, and later, full aileron application at high speed would almost put your helmet through the canopy!

Next was the barrel roll, after which it was time to show off a unique feature of the jet – the rotary bomb bay – during a hard turn. On a damp day, the vapours from the wing tips were as good as any specialist smoke dispensers. The aim was to roll the bomb door shut as the aircraft paralleled the crowd line, still in the hard turn. The fumble for the switch (below and lower than the throttles and exactly like the surrounding switches) at 5.5g, whilst looking over my right shoulder for crowd centre, placed a severe strain on one's manual dexterity.

Compared to the previous manoeuvre, you would think that an aileron roll would be quite straight forward, but not so. The rudder and aileron trims on the Buccaneer needed to be set precisely as to avoid a horrendous slashing of the nose during the roll. We learned this one at Mildenhall very early on in the season when we started the roll pointing along the display axis and finished up pointing 25° further right, ie at the crowd!. Luckily, a Canadian break manoeuvre is next, so by throwing it in a little earlier than normal we avoided flying over the assembled masses.

Hawker Siddeley Buccaneer S.2B

Type: Two-seat attack aircraft

Engines: Two 11,030 lb (5003 kg) Rolls-Royce RB.168-1A Spey 101 two-shaft turbofans

Dimensions: Span 44 ft (13.41 m); length 63 ft 5 in (19.33 m); height 16 ft 3 in (4.95 m); wing area 514.7 sq ft (47.82 m²)

Weights: Empty about 30,000 lb (13,610 kg); max loaded 62,000 lb (28,123 kg)

Performance: Max speed 645 mph (1038 km/h, Mach 0.85) at sea level; initial climb at 46,000 lb, 7000 ft (2134 m)/min; service ceiling over 40,000 ft (9144 m); range on typical Hi-Lo-Hi strike mission with weapon load, 2300 miles (3700 km)

Armament: Rotating bomb door carries four 1000 lb (454 kg) bombs, or multi-sensor reconnaissance pack, or 440 gal tank; four wing pylons each stressed to 3000 lb (1361 kg), compatible with very wide range of guided and/or free-fall missiles. Total internal and external stores load 16,000 lb (7257 kg)

Status: First S.2B for RAF flown 8 January 1970, with deliveries of 42 built to this standard continuing into 1976. All RAF S.2As and most ex-Royal Navy S.2s modified to B specs

The final fling was a low pass at around 530 kts and a pull-up to the vertical at 5.5g for a climbing roll, and roll off the top, peaking at around 10,000 to 11,000 ft. From above, the whole display site could be clearly seen. At Gibraltar towards the end of the season the view was absolutely magnificent. On other occasions I completed the recovery in cloud on instruments, which was not quite as spectacular!

In summary, there were no really 'wacky' manoeuvres in our routine, but then the uniqueness of displaying the aeroplane more than compensated for this, both for us in the cockpit and for the spectator on the ground. It gave us a real sense of satisfaction to perform a slick routine. I wouldn't have missed it for the world!

FROM THE BACK SEAT

Having joined the RAF on a sixth form scholarship scheme, I was entitled to 30 hrs flying at a civilian flying club. At the tender age of 17 I was zooming (at 100 kts) around the skies of Kent before I had even passed my driving test. Officer training followed a couple of years later, and by 1987 I was a fully qualified fast jet navigator. The mighty Buccaneer was to be my workhorse for the next six years.

So what did a display navigator do in the big Blackburn jet? Good question, as I had no stick or throttles in the back seat so my destiny was totally in the hands (well almost) of my trusty driver up front. As Neil explained earlier, the Buccaneer was definitely not an aerobatic aircraft, but flying it in a display sequence was certainly a challenge not worth missing.

The Buccaneer needed good crew co-operation to operate in its normal environment, and even more so during a display. We had no real HUD so I was required to do my impersonation of a talking altimeter and compass, thus allowing Neil to concentrate on the flying just that little bit more.

There was a lot of shouting and grunting between the two cockpits throughout the course of the season during our six-minute show, but we still talk to each other today. I was there primarily to give Neil his cues for each event within the display – for example when to roll out, when to pull up and when to leave the bar, or hospitality tent, and go to bed. As well as all this, as navigator it was my job to make sure we arrived at the correct time, and more importantly at the correct airfield.

The season was great fun despite all the hard work, and to display the last real British bomber across the UK in its final year was both an honour and a privilege for Neil and myself. We will certainly miss the old girl.

RIGHT: Blackburn built the Buccaneer to last – just look at the size of the main undercarriage legs. Acting as extremely effective airbrakes in this instance, the extended gear has allowed Neil Benson to creep ever closer to the Hercules photoship as the pair cruise over the Moray Firth. The crew flew almost all of No 208 Sqn's Buccaneers at some point during the season, alternating between camouflaged and all-grey jets depending on which aircraft was serviceable at the time (Photo by Duncan Cubitt)

BELOW RIGHT: In previous seasons the display crew hailed from No 12 Sqn, who shared Lossiemouth with No 208 until October 1993, when the former unit replaced its S.2Bs with Tornado GR.1s. To mark the occasion of the impending retirement of the Buccaneer from the RAF, No 1 Group put aloft a pair of jets from each of the squadrons and had them formate with a media-packed Hercules C.1 that had flown up specially for the event from Lyneham. Exhibiting flashes of colour from all three of the schemes worn by the Buccaneer force over the past four years, XX885 leads its traditionally camouflaged squadron mate as the section cruises off the starboard side of the Hercules. Nicknamed 'Famous Grouse / Caroline / Hello Sailor' during the Gulf War, this 20-year-old veteran flew missions and destroyed an Antonov An-12 during its tour of duty (Photo by Duncan Cubitt)

ABOVE: The distinctive unofficial unit enblem of No 208 Sqn

Jaguar GR.1A No16(R) Squadron

Flt Lt Andy Cubin

'READY?' came Gary's voice over the R/T. It was a windy autumn afternoon at RAF Lossiemouth as we held the Jaguar T.2 on the brakes at the end of runway 23. I was sitting in the back about to experience my first Jaguar display, with Gary Miller in the front showing me the ropes. He had just finished a season as the Jaguar display pilot, and I had been fortunate to be considered as his successor – this sortie would act as the official look-see!

Gary hacked his stopwatch and released the brakes. The aircraft leaped forward with an acceleration like I had never experienced before. Normal internal fuel is 3200 kg, but the display load is only 1600 kg and within what seemed a blink of an eye, our Jaguar lifted off at 150 kts. Almost immediately, the ground seemed to be scraping against the right wing as we threw on 60° of bank at 100 ft, pulled to 60° off the runway heading and pitched rather coarsely to 40° above the horizon . . .

The next seven minutes were a blur of rolls and hard 'g' turns whilst Gary calmly talked me through his sequence and I struggled to keep up with what was going on. I had flown the Jaguar for nine years and had amassed some 2200 hours on type. During that time I had operated the aircraft both over the Arctic wastes of northern Norway in the depths of winter, and in the blistering heat over the deserts of the Middle East, so I thought I'd seen it all! Walking away from the T.2 after our display, I remember being deep in thought; I'd never seen the aeroplane handled like that and I was very impressed.

I had been under the impression that you just got airborne, rushed past the crowd upside down a few times with a couple of wacky dumb-bell wing-overs at either end, and that was it! That was when I started to feel guilty. Flying the display obviously required considerable skill, and I found myself envious of that skill which I didn't possess. I felt very proud and also very humble when I was selected to take over as the Jaguar Display Pilot.

For the next few months, I put a lot of work into constructing a new sequence. The old display, although good, had been the same for several seasons, and there was a strong feeling within the squadron that changes should be made. Therein lay the problem; how to best display the aircraft bearing in mind its handling and performance limitations?

Taking a look at the Jaguar, it can soon be seen that it is an aircraft designed for high-speed flight. It is small and streamlined, with a thin supersonic-type wing. In fact, the wing span is only 28 ft, has a low aspect ratio and is shoulder-mounted on the fuselage. These characteristics give the Jaguar a superbly stable ride at high speed and low-level, even in turbulent conditions. Unfortunately, these characteristics do not lend themselves to what is really needed in display flying – turning ability.

This is why the display is the shape it is. By necessity, the passes in front of the crowd need to be separated by what seem to be very large wing-overs and Derry dumb-bells at either end. I therefore concentrated primarily on changing the things that would occur directly in front of the crowd.

I started by looking at the aircraft itself. Hundreds of man-hours had gone into the paint scheme to give the Jaguar its distinctive appearance and surely that deserved some recognition. An ordinary photo fly-by was incorporated, running down the crowd-line using 45° of bank, but holding the aircraft straight with full top rudder. This, when seen from the ground, shows off the Jaguar's colour scheme and is the perfect opportunity for the thousands of aviation photographers found at air displays to get some decent shots.

The slow roll, high-speed run and slow-speed fly-by had to stay, as did the max rate turn, but I introduced a few subtle changes in between. The max rate turn is now entered from inverted at 420 kts. The higher speed allows greater nose authority at the beginning of the turn to compensate for the latter half where I have to back off on the pull to achieve the required speed for the final manoeuvre.

This has to be carefully flown as the aircraft is close to the edge of its flying envelope, and smoothness is the key at this stage. The aircraft is pitched up at relatively slow speed to as close to the vertical as possible, before being rolled 90° away from the crowd to position for the final landing.

There is a lot to cram into a seven-minute display slot – it is a mental as well as a physical exercise and can be quite exhausting, but from a professional point of view, a very satisfying expe-

ABOVE: A series of stunning publicity shots of the 'black cat' were taken early on in the season by RAF photographer, Sgt Rick Brewell, who cleverly used the rugged coastline around Lossiemouth as a canvas against which to pose the Jaguar. From this angle the jet's lustreless finish is readily apparent, which contrasted markedly with the glossy scheme worn by the Hawks from Valley and Chivenor (Photo by Sgt Rick Brewell via Flt Lt Andy Cubin)

RIGHT: The highly coveted position of 1994 display pilot is filled by seasoned Jaguar exponent, Flt Lt Andy Cubin. An accomplished veteran with nine years and 2200 hours on-type, he has flown the jet across the globe in both war and peace *(Photo by John Ingham via Flt Lt Andy Cubin)*

BELOW: One drawback associated with the Jaguar is its lack of a built-in ladder, the problem being compounded by the jet's stalky undercarriage. Here, Gary Miller has enlisted the help of a Land Rover, suitably manoeuvred alongside the jet's cockpit. This unusual shot was taken at the 1993 RAF Leeming open day

BELOW: Early on in the season Gary made use of a more conventionally camouflaged Jaguar whilst his 'black cat' was being prepared following a major overhaul at St Athan, in Wales. Surrounded by safety vehicles and courtesy cars, the pilot taxies out at the beginning of his display during the Fighter Meet at North Weald in May 1993. At the same event two years before, the solo routine flown by the 1991 Jaguar display pilot won the highly prized John Watt Memorial Trophy *(Photo by John Dibbs)*

rience. I am very privileged to do what I do. I fly between 30 to 40 displays a year for two seasons, and each venue is different and requires unique planning. A mountain of administrative preparation work has to be tackled also.

Despite the hard work, the job is tremendously rewarding. Aside from the sheer thrill of flying a combat aircraft to the extreme of its performance envelope, the stimulus provided by the small group of fellow display pilots who are all dedicated to finding perfection in their flying is equally inspiring. Continuously striving to do better is all part and parcel of the flying game.

Asked if I would swap? Not even for a packet of DAZ!!

Sepecat Jaguar GR.1A

Countries of Origin: France and United Kingdom

Type: Single-seat tactical strike fighter

Powerplant: Two 4620 lb (2100 kg) dry and 7140 lb (3240 kg) reheat Rolls-Royce Turbomeca RT.172 Adour 102 turbofans

Performance: (At typical weight) Max speed, 820 mph (1320 km/h) or Mach 1.1 at 1000 ft (303 m), 1057 mph (1700 km/h) or Mach 1.6 at 32,810 ft (10,000 m); cruise with max ordnance, 430 mph (690 km/h) or Mach 0.65 at 39,370 ft (12,000 m); range with external fuel for lo-lo-lo mission profile, 450 miles (724 km), for Hi-Lo-Hi mission profile, 710 miles (1142 km); ferry range, 2270 miles (3650 km)

Weights: Normal take-off, 23,000 lb (10,430 kg); max take-off, 32,600 lb (14,790 kg)

Armament: Two 30 mm Aden cannon and up to 10,000 lb (4536 kg) ordnance on five external hardpoints

Status: First of eight prototypes flown 8 September 1968. First production Jaguar E for France flown 2 November 1971, with first Jaguar A following 20 April 1972. First production Jaguar S for UK flown 11 October 1972. RAF received a total of 202 aircraft

Dimensions: Span, 28 ft 6 in (8.69 m); length, 50 ft 11 in (15.52 m); height, 16 ft 0½ in (4.89 m); wing area, 260.3 sq ft (24.18 m²)

Tornado GR.1A No II(AC) Squadron

Sqn Ldr Steve Cockram – Pilot Flt Lt Tim Robinson – Navigator
Flt Lt Eddie Middleton – Navigator

BELOW RIGHT: From this angle there looks as if there is barely enough room in the cockpit of a Tornado GR.1A for a pair of Martin-Baker 10A ejection seats, let alone two crewmembers to sit in them. Separated by the seat back, firing rails and rear cockpit 'black boxes', pilot, Sqn Ldr Steve Cockram, and navigator, Flt Lt Eddie Middleton, pose in their No II(AC) Sqn jet at Newcastle Airport prior to performing over the Sunderland shoreline. Both highly seasoned Tornado aircrew with over 3700 hours on type between them, the pair only began flying displays together from July onwards following the departure of the original navigator, Flt Lt Tim Robinson, to Australia on an F-111 exchange posting. Eddie, the replacement, was chosen from No II(AC) Sqn's back-seater ranks primarily because he had already performed the job way back in 1984 whilst with No 27 Sqn

WHILST serving on *Operation Jural* at Royal Saudi Air Force base Dhahran in October 1992, the then Flt Lt Steve Cockram and Flt Lt Tim Robinson of No II(AC) Sqn were asked if they were interested in displaying the Tornado GR.1 for the 1993 season. As they obviously were, their names were submitted, along with six other crews from Nos 27 and 617 Sqns, to HQ No 1 Group for consideration by higher command.

In January 1993, the squadron was advised by No 1 Group that Flt Lts Cockram and Robinson had been chosen as the Tornado GR.1 display crew. Soon after, Flt Lt Robinson was told that he had been selected to join the Royal Australian Air Force on an F-111 exchange posting commencing in August of that same year. Fortunately, No II(AC) Sqn were able to provide a replacement navigator in the form of Flt Lt Eddie Middleton (who had

previously displayed the Tornado in 1984), and he filled the vacant back seat from July onwards.

Steve was promoted to squadron leader as the season began, and he was duly re-posted to No II(AC) Sqn as a Flight Commander, which allowed him to retain the airshow slot. Well qualified to display the Tornado GR.1 to its fullest capabilities, Steve has amassed over 1600 hours on type (out of a total of just over 2000 in his logbook) during the past six years, most of this 'stick time' being accrued whilst on tours with Nos 17(F) and 14 Sqns at Marham.

Flt Lt Robinson has over 1600 hours on Tornados, achieved with Nos 20 and II(AC) Sqns whilst the units were based at RAF Laarbruch in Germany. He returned to Marham with the latter squadron following service in the Gulf War. His replacement, Flt Lt Middleton, boasts 1700 hours plus on Tornados, and has previously

ABOVE: Despite HQ No 1 Group approving a special scheme for the squadron's designated display jet, heavy operational commitments with the UN's force in Saudi Arabia early on in the season precluded its adoption. Therefore, all performances were flown in a routine line Tornado GR.1A from the unit's Marham base. Photographed here under leadened Wiltshire skies, this jet is having to pick its way through the typically congested taxyways at Fairford on arrival day in search of its allocated spot in the static park. Mounted on the outer wing pylon is the almost mandatory BOZ 100 chaff/flare dispenser (Photo by Tony Holmes)

served with No 27 Sqn at Marham, with the Tactical Weapons Conversion Unit (RAF Honington) as an instructor, and at MoD (Procurement Executive) on the Air-launched Anti-Radiation Missile (ALARM) tnals in America, before arriving on No II(AC) Sqn at the end of 1992.

THE DISPLAY SEQUENCE

The crew decided from the outset to fly the aircraft in as clean a configuration as possible. Outboard stores – the BOZ chaff/flare dispenser and Sky Shadow ECM pod – were retained to reduce aircraft fatigue during a display, but this in turn reduced the amount of negative 'g' available and precluded manoeuvres such as inverted flying, slow and hesitation rolls.

The original display routine was fairly long, with many aerobatic manoeuvres. Unfortunately, as the Tornado is not an agile aircraft, the routine used a lot of airspace and was considered unsuitable for public viewing. However, by reducing the speed of many of the manoeuvres, the overall performance appeared much tighter, so 300 kts was used as the basis for most of the display. This was further reduced to 200 kts for the undercarriage down pass and 'cranked up' to 550 for the display finale.

A total of three sequences were approved to cater for the vague British summers. The Rolling

and Flat shows took five-and-a-half minutes to perform, whilst the Full routines ran for a minute longer. Should a take-off and landing have been required then up to a further four minutes had to be added to each display.

Every performance had to be flown in the same direction, which therefore forced the pilot to pull hard into a left turn immediately after launch – this restriction was a nuisance to the crew all season, and they have recommended that in future displays should be cleared to be flown in both directions.

When involved in performing the routine itself, the crew felt that they had experienced few differences between normal operations and display flying. On the topic of his back-seater, Steve believes that the mark of a good navigator is someone who tells the pilot what he needs to know just before he asks the question. In this respect he has been fortunate to fly with two of the most capable navigators on the Tornado GR.1 force.

To try and explain the way a crew work together during a performance is quite difficult to put into words, but maybe a good description is that the navigator acts like the pilot's conscience! A common belief is that the navigator must also be mad.

Due to unforeseen difficulties in the early part

ABOVE: Devoid of stores and carrying enough fuel internally to perform its very noisy full show, the GR.1A is manoeuvred onto Cranfield's main runway using the aircraft's effective nose-wheel steering. The Tornado was built with a wide-track undercarriage, which is very forgiving on landing. The aircraft has an impressive shortfield capability thanks to thrust reverser plates which swing down over the jet pipes and deflect the jet wash upwards and forwards *(Photo by Cliff Knox)*

of the season, the crew displayed almost entirely from their home station at Marham. However, from July onwards they were able to get away to most venues and stay 'overnight' away from base if necessary.

As a result of the early-season problems that forced the crew to undertake displays near to Marham, only two overseas events were attended; one at Eindhoven in Holland and the other at Hradec Kralove in the Czech Republic – Steve and Eddie have fond memories of the the latter venue!

The 1993 season was a highly successful one for No II(AC) Sqn's 'display team', and both Steve and Eddie are hoping to fill the display slot again in 1994 .

Panavia Tornado GR.1

Dimensions: Span (max) 45 ft 8 in (13.90 m), (min) 28 ft 2.5 in (8.59 m); area 322.9 sq ft (300.00 m²), length and height 54 ft 9.5 in (16.70 m), 18 ft 8½ in (5.70 m)

Powerplant: Two Turbo-Union RB.199-34R-4 Mk 101 turbofans, each rated at 8500 lbs dry and 15,000 lbs in afterburner

Weights: Empty 28,000 lbs (12,700 kg); loaded (clean) 40,000 lbs (18,145 kg); max take-off weight 55,000 lbs (25,000 kg)

Speed: Max speed (clean) 840 mph (1350 km/h) at 500 ft (150 m), or Mach 1.1/1385 mph (2230 km/h) at 36,900 ft (11,000 m)

Range: Tactical radius (Lo-Lo-Lo) with external stores 450 miles (725 km), or (Hi-Lo-Hi) with external stores 750 miles (1200 km)

Armament: Two 27 mm Mauser cannon, plus provision for up to 19,840 lb (9000 kg) of disposable stores carried on seven external stores

Status: Developed by consortium of manufacturers from Britain, Italy and West Germany, first Tornado IDS flew in August 1974. GR.1 began to enter RAF service in 1980

Tornado F.3 No 56(R) Squadron

Flt Lt Jerry Goatham – Pilot   Flt Lt Paul Brown – Navigator

AT ANY airshow, the fast jet displays have always been renowned as show-stoppers. The fairground attractions and the ice cream stalls suddenly lose their appeal as modern military aircraft are put through their paces in the skies above. I can remember on many occasions as a young boy walking around yet another airshow wishing it could be me up there displaying in front of the public, showing what the aircraft was capable of. So it was a great day when my squadron commander, Wg Cdr Pete Coker (the 'Boss'), informed the unit in early January that RAF Coningsby, and more specifically, our squadron, was to provide the Tornado F.3 display for the 1993 and 94 seasons.

I had joined the RAF in 1981 as a Simulator Technician before being commissioned as an officer in 1984. After initial flying training, I was posted to fly the new Tornado F.2, soon to become the F.3, as one of the first ab initio pilots. After completing the course at No 229 Operational Conversion Unit (OCU), I joined No 5 Sqn at RAF Coningsby in 1988. In 1992, having finished my first tour, I returned to the F.3 OCU, now designated No 56(Reserve) Sqn as an instructor. It was from this posting that I was able to fulfil my ambition to become a fast jet display pilot.

The receipt of the news that No 56(R) Sqn was to perform the F.3 display meant that all the pilots who hoped to be selected for the prize slot had to undergo a rigorous selection procedure. Each was tasked with producing a display sequence which he then had to fly with the 'Boss' in the back seat, before being interviewed by the Station Commander. I was lucky enough to be selected as the display pilot, with Flt Lt Paul Brown, a close friend and colleague, as my display navigator. Paul had joined the RAF in 1985 after completing a physics degree at Oxford University. He attended the same OCU course as me, and also joined No 5 Sqn in 1988. He moved back to No 56(R) Sqn in 1991 and became a Qualified Weapons Instructor on the Tornado F.3.

The countdown for the 1993 season began in February when both Paul and I started designing our sequences. The display had to be exciting to watch and as professional as possible, so the sequences were designed with three main aims in mind. Firstly, and most importantly, we wanted to display the F.3's strengths in the display environment. The jet does not have the inherent agility of the MiG-29 *Fulcrum* or Mirage 2000, but it is extremely fast, noisy, and by combining the variable-geometry wing sweep with a respectable turn radius at low-level, is able to exploit its advantages over other modern fighters.

Secondly, the display was designed to appeal to the general public, not the minority of aircrew critics who inhabit the beer tent! Finally, the sequence had to be relatively simple and easy to fly as this was our first season as the display crew. These aims were fulfilled by not necessarily flying professionally difficult manoeuvres, but by flying low and fast, utilising the aesthetic appeal of the F.3 and linking the sequence with a routine of academic aerobatic manoeuvres. If the resulting noise level could

ABOVE:
Although the pair initially flew a 'vanilla' F.3 on the circuit early on in the season, by Mildenhall they had unveiled their spectacularly decorated ZE839, resplendent in full No 56(R) Sqn markings. Much polishing was undertaken by the unit's groundcrew throughout the season on the jet's distinctive blood red tail as it tended to blacken badly following a couple of short, thrust reverser-assisted landings (Photo by John

bring a halt to all conversation, so much the better! Two other fundamental rules were also taken into consideration during the initial stages of designing the sequence – keep it as close to the audience as possible (within safety regulations) and never fly straight and level between manoeuvres.

Although the sequence only lasted eight minutes, months of preparation had gone into planning the display to ensure that it met the aims that we had set ourselves. I spent many hours reading post display season reports, post accident reports and seeking advice from any squadron personnel with previous experience of the display environment. The latter was available in abundance at Coningsby as it is also the home of the Battle of Britain Memorial Flight (BBMF), and consequently has many aircrew with display experience. In addition, the previous Tornado F.3 display pilot was now on No 5 Sqn and he was able to show me 'tricks of the trade' which he had learnt during the previous two years.

Once the sequence had been designed it was then time to take to the air to see if it actually worked. Initially the routine was flown at a base height of 5000 ft.

LEFT: Many of the RAF's greatest pilots have flown the service's premier fighter in the public domain, men of the calibre of Broadhurst, Tuck, Malan and Black. In 1993, the names of Flt Lts Jerry Goatham (pilot) and Paul Brown (navigator) were added to the list. Both QFIs at Coningsby with No 56(R) Sqn, the pair brought their considerable experience of flying the Tornado F.3 in frontline service to bear when they planned their routine for the summer season. Knowing that their aircraft was not as agile as an F-16 or a Mirage 2000, Jerry and Paul focused on the jet's strengths – its speed, stability at low-level, aesthetic appeal and audible dominance *(Photo by John Dibbs)*

made to the display to make it look as exciting as possible for a real crowd with a real

The proposed sequence was then forwarded to Headquarters 11 Group at RAF Bentley Priory for approval by the Air Officer Commanding (AOC), Air Vice Marshal John Allison CBE, a highly experienced display pilot in his own right. Once approval had been given, supervision of the display work-up was passed to Gp Capt Andy Williams AFC, Coningsby's Station Commander, who is also an experienced ex-BBMF display pilot.

The squadron deployment to RAF Akrotiri in Cyprus during 1993 provided the perfect opportunity to rehearse the sequence in ideal weather conditions, thus allowing us to work down to the 'hard deck' height of 500 ft much quicker. Throughout this period, minor adjustments were

display line and centre point. Surprisingly, what feels good in the air doesn't always look good from the ground! However, thorough debriefs and inputs from the Station Commander and the 'Boss' helped to refine the sequence.

On our return to the UK, our next hurdle was to display in front of the AOC on 20 April. If he had felt that the routine was not quite ready then we would have been required to continue with further practice, before displaying once again for him. All went well on the day, and approval was granted to display the F.3 in public. Now the hard work would really begin in earnest!

THE DISPLAY

Depending on the weather at the individual airshow venues our display would follow one of three sequences. These were:

The Full Sequence – this was a full aerobatic display involving manoeuvres in the looping and rolling planes. It required a minimum cloud base of 5000 ft and good visibility.

The Rolling Sequence – this was flown when the cloud base was too low for looping manoeuvres but good enough for aerobatics in the rolling plane.

The Flat Sequence – this was a flat performance flown when the conditions were outside those covered above but within safety limits.

A full show, where the crowd was to the right of the aircraft during the take-off run or low overshoot, would have taken the following format:

● **1.** The display would start from take-off or a low overshoot in the landing configuration. At 170 kts the aircraft would be racked into a tight climbing turn whilst selecting gear up. Leaving maximum reheat power and mid-flaps selected, the minimum radius turn would be established at 240 kts, 4g and 300 ft with the stick fully back.

● **2.** The turn would be continued to 50° off at crowd left. The aircraft would then be accelerated to 290 kts before an aggressive 4.5g pull through 45° nose up would be executed for a Derry wing over. The aircraft would top at about 3500 ft, allowing the crew to check the actual cloudbase, and would then be pulled round to point down the crowd line.

● **3.** The next manoeuvre would be to fly the aircraft inverted at 320 kts from right to left, culminating in a 4.5g pull up through 70°. This would be followed by a roll through 180° for a half Cuban 8, topping at 5000 ft above ground level.

● **4.** On return to crowd centre a Canadian break would then be performed, leading into a maximum rate turn at 330 kts. This would be flown at 5.5 to 6g and at 500 ft. The turn would be continued to 50° off crowd line for a further Derry wing over before leading into a slow roll flown from right to left at 360 kts.

● **5.** The aircraft would then begin a hesitation Derry turn. During the turn the aircraft would be decelerated to 220 kts, the undercarriage lowered at 235 kts and the wings swept fully back to 67°.

● **6.** A 'dirty' slow speed pass would then be flown from left to right at 220 kts and 200 ft. Then the burners and gear would be selected and the aircraft accelerated to 250 kts, the wings being swept forward to 25° at the same time. At 250 kts the aircraft would be pitched up for a half horizontal 8 topping at 4500 ft. From this the aircraft would be pulled to 60° nose down before rolling through 180° at 3000 ft.

● **7.** On retaining crowd left the aircraft would be pulled into a 270° turn whilst accelerating to 350 kts, with the aim being to roll out pointing at crowd centre. The aircraft would then be pitched into the vertical using 5.5g to show the underside in plan form. This manoeuvre would continue into a half clover topping at 5000 ft, which would be concluded by passing left to right.

● **8.** From this an accelerating hesitation Derry turn followed by a four-point hesitation roll would be flown from right to left at 400 kts. The aircraft would enter its final Derry wing over at crowd left whilst accelerating to 450 kts and sweeping the wings back to 67°.

● **9.** The final pass would be flown at 100 ft and 600 kts/0.92 Mach. At crowd right the aircraft would be pitched into the vertical using 7g to finish with a vertical roll departure. The usual height achieved by the aircraft during this manoeuvre would be 24,000 ft.

THE SEASON

There is much more to displaying a fast jet than just pitching up on the day, flying around for a few minutes and retiring to the hospitality tent. Initially, a list of airshow dates arrived from the Ministry of Defence Participation Committee; this provided us with our first real insight into where we would be spending much of the summer. In addition to the expected venues such as Mildenhall, Finningley, Leuchars and, Coningsby, there were shows in Jersey, Sweden, Austria and Gibraltar which were particularly welcomed.

A groundcrew team was selected from volunteers within the squadron, and fellow instructors placed their bids to fly the spare aircraft (in case of serviceability problems with the main jet) to the venues so that they could enjoy a weekend away. Once we had received the dates we could formulate a general plan for the display season. The programme was studied, and we paid particularly close attention to weekends where more than one display had to be performed. Decisions such as where to base the aircraft and the groundcrew had to be made.

We found that for every plan, there had to be a back up, particularly to cater for the idiosyncrasies of the British weather! A lesson we

RIGHT: Wings swept fully-forward, and with the jet carrying a solitary Sidewinder acquisition round under its starboard pylon, Jerry pushes the throttle forward and ignites the twin afterburners, leaving the photographer (strapped in his Yak-11 cameraship) firmly in the Tornado's warm wake. The 'loud pedal' is regularly used throughout the crew's routine, allowing the pilot to keep up with his pre-determined manoeuvre times, as well as send an audible shiver down the spines of the assembled crowd. The twin Turbo-Union RB.199 turbofans are each rated at 17,000 lbs of thrust in afterburner, which will propel the F.3 to speeds in excess of Mach 2 *(Photo by John Dibbs)*

learnt very quickly was 'never assume – check'.

One of the busiest weekends of the 1993 season was during July, with displays at RNAS Yeovilton, Bruntingthorpe and RAF Church Fenton. The weekend began with a transit from Coningsby to Yeovilton in company with the spare F.3 to arrive by 1400 on the Friday. On our arrival we were able to carry out a visual check of the display site from the air, paying particular attention to built up areas, high ground and airfield obstructions. Seeing the display area for real, and not just from an ordinance survey map or aerial photograph, was particularly helpful.

On landing, the groundcrew, who had arrived earlier by road, received the aircraft for refuelling and routine servicing. I then briefed the groundcrew chief on any changes to the original plan, including the nominated airframe for the Saturday display. Paul and the spare crew went in search of the aircrew reception area to sort out accommodation details and meal tickets, and to check the time of the pre-arranged social function.

The Saturday morning began at an extremely early hour to allow for a quick breakfast before getting on the road to Yeovilton ahead of the traffic jams. There is no point in being a display crew if, at your appointed slot time, you're still on the approach road surrounded by thousands of cars queuing for the parking areas. The flight brief was then held at 0900 hrs, and it gave us the opportunity to discuss the display with pilots from the preceding and succeeding slots.

This was particularly important since most events like to run to schedule, and a fairly large and fast aircraft preceding a small and slow one needs close co-ordination. On this day, particular attention had to be paid to the weather, especially cloud conditions for the transit to Bruntingthorpe since the civil airfield had no radar or navigational aids, and therefore our transit would have to be under visual flight rules (VFR).

At most displays Paul and I brief one hour and 10 minutes prior to take-off. The briefing is of particular importance for a two-seat fast jet display as close co-operation is required between the pilot and navigator to ensure that the flight runs smoothly. Consideration has to be given to display lines, show centre and the large visual cues that can be utilised, as well as ensuring that specific datum headings and wind compensation have been correctly analysed. The brief also provides an opportunity to talk through the sequence in slow time, and we discuss the full display, with rolling as a back up bearing in mind the average summer day in the UK is 3/8ths cloud at 2500-

RIGHT: The kneepad notes used as visual cues by Flt Lt Jerry Goatham during the course of a display

BELOW: This detailed diagram depicts all the manoeuvres flown by the F.3 crew during a Full display

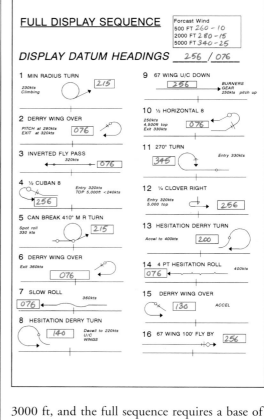

3000 ft, and the full sequence requires a base of 5000 ft. Gate heights are re-emphasised and noted down by Paul.

Finally, holding patterns are covered, together with timing from the hold to the start point. Following the 30-minute brief, I sign the Form 700 for the primary display aircraft and the spare, and carry out an external check for both aircraft. Once completed, we then strap into the primary aircraft, start up the auxiliary power unit (APU) and check in with the display co-ordinator on the pre-briefed frequency to ensure that the display is running to schedule.

Simultaneously, the spare crew power up the second F.3 to ensure that it is ready should a malfunction occur on the primary airframe. Engines are started 30 minutes before take-off, allowing both of us sufficient time to check out all the systems. Ten minutes before our planned take-off time, we taxy to the ground holding point, where we complete our pre-launch checks. Usually, we recap the sequence we are about to fly, stressing any compensation required for that particular venue.

The Yeovilton display was a success, and we taxied the aircraft to the waiting fuel bowser. On this particular day, because of our scheduled departure to Bruntingthorpe, there was no time to waste, so as the aircraft was refuelled and serviced, the crews discussed the transit to the next venue and walked to the individual aircraft.

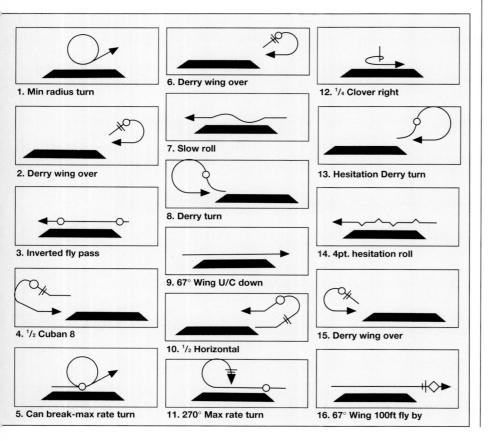

1. Min radius turn
2. Derry wing over
3. Inverted fly pass
4. ½ Cuban 8
5. Can break-max rate turn
6. Derry wing over
7. Slow roll
8. Derry turn
9. 67° Wing U/C down
10. ½ Horizontal
11. 270° Max rate turn
12. ¼ Clover right
13. Hesitation Derry turn
14. 4pt. hesitation roll
15. Derry wing over
16. 67° Wing 100ft fly by

ABOVE: Few modern combat aircraft look as stunning as a No 56(R) Sqn F.3 crackling through the heavens with its wings fully swept at an angle of 67°. Jerry ends his routine with a 100 ft pass over the runway in this configuration, which enables him to achieve Mach 0.92 with only judicious use of the afterburner. At crowd right he pulls the control column back into the pit of his stomach and grunts heavily to avoid blacking out as the F.3 endures a 7g pitch up and is vertically rolled to a height of 24,000 ft, thus ending another successful display (Photo by John Dibbs)

Sunday had its own peculiarities – a transit from Bruntingthorpe to Church Fenton in less than ideal weather, a display commencing with an overshoot, not a take-off, and the recovery to Bruntingthorpe.

The weather was of particular concern on this day since it forced us to transit VFR below cloud in an environment busy with light aircraft and microlights, which necessitated an extremely vigilant lookout and radar search. Luckily, Sunday morning proceeded as advertised and the F.3 was back on the ground at Bruntingthorpe with sufficient time to allow us to take lunch in the participants' tent (without a doubt the best on the circuit so far).

Extra preparation was required for the brief as I had to consult with the display pilot displaying after the F.3 regarding our planned recovery to the airfield. We normally conclude our F.3 routine with a vertical departure, and since it takes about two minutes to reposition for a visual run in and break, following our finale it is desirable to hold off and let the next aircraft in the programme perform its display.

This also allows the noise level to drop before the F.3 rushes in at 600 kts and 100 ft for a 'burner' break. To that end, co-ordination between display aircraft is essential. Following the Bruntingthorpe performance, the F.3 was handed over to the groundcrew who prepared it for the short transit flight back to RAF Coningsby the

following morning, ready for its weekday flying.

All that remains to be done at this stage of a display is to inform the co-ordinator of our planned departure time from the venue, and to reflect on the weekend over a beer or two, before beginning to think about the next airshow. □

Panavia Tornado F.3

Country of Origin: United Kingdom

Type: Tandem two-seat air defence interceptor

Powerplant: Two (approx) 9000 lb st (4082 kgp) dry and 17,000 lb st (7711 kgp) reheat Turbo-Union RB.199-34R Mk 104 turbofans

Performance: (Estimated) Max speed, 920 mph (1480 km/h) or Mach 1.2 at sea level, 1450 mph (2333 km/h) or Mach 2.2 at 40,000 ft (12,190 m); time to 30,000 ft (9145 m), 1.7 min; operational radius (combat air patrol with two 330 Imp gal/1500 l drop tanks and allowance for 2 hrs loiter), 350-450 miles (560-725 km); ferry range (with four 330 Imp gal/1400 l external tanks), 2650 miles (4265 km)

Weights: (Estimated) Empty equipped, 31,970 lb (14 500 kg); normal loaded (four Sky Flash and four AIM-9L AAMs), 50,700 lb (30 000 kg); max, 56,000 lb (25,400 kg)

Armament: One 27 mm IWKA-Mauser cannon plus four BAe Sky Flash and four AIM-9L Sidewinder AAMs

Status: First of three F.2 prototypes flown on 27 October 1979, and first of 18 production F.2s (including six F.2Ts) flown 5 March 1984. Deliveries of F.3s (against RAF requirement for 147) commenced in 1986

Dimensions: Span (25° sweep), 45 ft 7^1/$_4$ in (13.90 m), (67° sweep), 28 ft 2^1/$_2$ in (8.59 m); Length, 59 ft 3 in (18.06 m); height, 18 ft 8 ^{1}/$_2$ in (5.70 m); wing area, 322.9 sq ft (30.00 m²)

DUBAI 93

O N TUESDAY 2 November I boarded the British Airways flight that would take me direct from London to Dubai. My journey would be rather more comfortable and relaxing than that undertaken by the Harrier pilots from RAF Laarbruch, in Germany, who had been chosen to ferry the two GR.7s to Dubai on my behalf. Their journey began on 3 November, and consisted of two five-hour sorties, broken by an overnight stop in Akrotiri, Cyprus. The Harriers formed part of a package which included two Tornado GR.1s from RAF Marham, a Hercules (containing the 21 Harrier and Tornado groundcrew, together with equipment and spares) and leading the trail, a VC10 tanker, which would be used frequently for air-to-air refuelling.

I would have happily flown one of the Harriers to Dubai myself, but was prevented from doing so by the requirement to carry out a practice display on the day the aircraft arrived – not a very sensible idea for a 'saddle-sore' pilot following a five-hour transit flight.

At Heathrow, and on my flight, I was amazed by the number of business men and women from all over Europe and America that were heading for the Middle East to participate in the exhibition. This was because the Dubai event was rather different from any of the other airshows which I had attended as it was a trade and exhibition fayre, not open to the public, at which major aviation related companies would be looking to outbid their competitors for a share of the region's aerospace business. All of the world's top aircraft manufacturer's would be present – Boeing, Airbus Industries, McDonnell Douglas etc, as well as a number of other less well known, but rapidly expanding, companies from Russia, South Africa,

BELOW: The GR.7 shared the display ramp at Dubai with some of the world's most modern combat types, including former potential adversaries like the Sukhoi Su-35 (left) and Su-27UB (right) *Flankers*. Photographed soon after its water injection tank had been refilled, the Harrier GR.7 is closely guarded by a member of the Dubai security forces whilst a No 20(R) Sqn maintainer gets to grips with an electrical problem immediately above him!

Asia and America. Even my participation was sponsored by industry, British Aerospace picking up the tab for the expenses incurred by the Harrier and Tornado teams. And with so much international interest, the media had flocked to the scene, setting up mobile press offices, remote TV broadcasting networks and publication and printing cells to produce daily bulletins and releases.

From the flying point of view, the show should have been no different from any other, apart from the heat. Unfortunately, the maximum weight at which the aircraft will hover is strongly influenced by the ambient temperature and air pressure. A fall in the latter by ten millibars or a temperature rise of just one degree will reduce the maximum hovering weight by approximately 150 lbs. I was therefore all too aware that with forecast temperatures as high as 30°C, the aircraft was not going to perform as well as I was used to. Having calculated the exact performance margins in the UK, and discussed the problem with Sqn Ldr Don Tanner, the Senior Engineering Officer (SENGO) of No 20(R) Sqn, we

elected to reduce the aircraft's all up weight by removing the intermediate and outer pylons, a saving of 500 lbs. It was also decided that on arrival in Dubai, the aircraft's air-to-air refuelling probe would be temporarily removed, saving a further 100 lbs. However, even these drastic measures would only partially compensate for the reduction in thrust caused by the higher temperatures. It was going to be an interesting display.

A day to myself in Dubai enabled me to sort out hotel accommodation, transport and smaller details such as show entry passes and briefing times. It was still very hot, temperatures soaring above the seasonal average into the high 30s. However, without the jets, there was nothing to do but wait.

Thursday saw the arrival of the aircraft. I had already been allocated a practice display slot (display times being pre-booked to ensure deconfliction from the incessant international movements) and was required to fly within an hour of the Harriers' arrival. The Hercules, complete with engineers, was not expected until the evening, so I was

ABOVE: Fellow display pilots sharing the live ramp with Rob hailed from all the main air forces and manufacturers from across the globe. In this dramatic view, the No 20(R) Sqn groundcrew endure the heat expelled from the idling SNECMA turbofan engine buried within the Mirage 2000-5, parked in front of the GR.7

RIGHT: Dozens of Arab dignatories were the briefed on the Harrier during the show, Rob being ably assisted in this task by a handful of fellow GR.7 pilots from Germany. This high ranking individual hails from Saudi Arabia, and he is being talked through the jet's unique V/STOL cockpit controls by Flt Lt Pete Squires from No 3 Sqn at Laarbruch

pleased to hear that both jets were serviceable.

A quick top up with fuel, and then I was ready to begin my first practice. From the word go, I could feel the lack of performance – it was if I was displaying with two 1000-lb bombs aboard. Although I had expected problems in the jetborne regime, I was surprised by the affect on the wing-borne manoeuvres. Usually I enter the max-rate turn at 400 kts, pull to the light buffet and finish the manoeuvre at the same speed. On this occasion, however, I found that I was rapidly losing energy, and half way round the turn, seeing the speed reducing through 350 kts, I had to relax my pull to prevent any further loss of energy, accepting the reduced rate of turn.

Fortunately, the jetborne manoeuvring worked as planned, and I found that by increasing the speed of the mini-circuit (to provide more wing lift), using a maximum of half a breaking stop when decelerating to the hover, decreasing the size of control deflections when initiating sideways and backwards flight, and wherever possible, minimising engine bleed, I was able to perform the complete sequence.

Talking to the other display pilots after the event, I was reassured by similar tales of woe. For example, the Tornado crew had been forced to use much more afterburner than usual, resulting

ABOVE: As his display slot approaches, Rob 'straps on' his GR.7 in preparation for yet another performance. Watching proceedings from ramp level is No 20(R) Sqn's Senior Engineering Officer, Sqn Ldr Don Tanner, a highly experienced Harrier man who, throughout the 1993 display season, proved invaluable in keeping the team airworthy with fully serviceable aircraft. Kitted out in full tropical KDs (Khaki Drill), Don has firmly lodged a finger in each ear to block out the deafening roar of the Su-27 performing almost directly above him (Photo by Cpl Bunce)

in the consumption of over 1000 lbs of additional fuel. Other pilots commented on the reduction of available 'g', and the increased size of their display manoeuvres. Nevertheless, despite feeling frustrated, everyone coped with the conditions.

The show began on Sunday 7 November, and ran for five consecutive days. Due to the actual show venue doubling as a busy international airport, the flying programme had to be restricted to two hours of displaying in the afternoon. Throughout this period the airport had to be closed to external traffic.

The list of participants was quite varied and included an Su-30/-35 pair, F-16, F/A-18, Mirage 2000, solo Su-27 and -35, a novel display of two Airbuses (A330 and 340), a number of Russian and Western helicopters, and several light trainers. It was interesting to note that most of the displays were not flown by squadron pilots, but by the company display pilots, keen to impress their audience in the hope of sales. For those watching from the comfort of their air conditioned chalets, the series of stunning displays must have been truly unforgettable.

At the beginning of the exhibition, the Harrier was scheduled to display in the middle of the flying programme, but by the end of the week, so popular was the aircraft that on the last day we were asked to close the show. However, circumstances were to dictate otherwise.

Although it was common knowledge that the

Dubai Airshow coincided with a visit by HRH Prince Charles to the Gulf, it was something of a surprise to discover that he would be spending a couple of hours at the exhibition, his visit overlapping with the first half hour of the flying display. Overnight, the Harrier moved to the beginning of the programme, enabling my last display of 1994 to be flown with a Royal audience. A suitably fiiting end to a highly enjoyable season. □

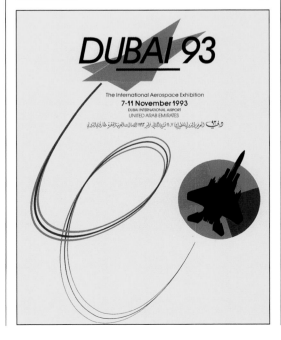

BRITISH AEROSPACE/ McDONNELL DOUGLAS HARRIER GR.7

1 Starboard all-moving tailplane
2 Tailplane composite construction
3 Tail missile warning radar
4 Missile Approach Warning radar equipment module
5 Tail pitch control air valve
6 Yaw control air valves
7 Tail 'bullet' fairing
8 Reaction control system air ducting
9 Rudder trim actuator
10 Rudder trim tab
11 Rudder composite construction
12 Rudder
13 Antenna
14 Fin-tip aerial fairing
15 Upper broad band communications antenna
16 Port tailplane
17 Graphite epoxy tailplane skin
18 Port side temperature probe
19 MAD compensator
20 Formation lighting strip
21 Fin construction
22 Fin attachment joint
23 Tailplane pivot sealing plate
24 Aerials
25 Ventral fin
26 Tail bumper
27 Lower broad band communications antenna
28 Tailplane hydraulic jack
29 Heat exchanger air exhaust
30 Aft fuselage frames
31 Rudder hydraulic actuator
32 Avionics equipment air conditioning plant
33 Avionics equipment racks
34 Heat exchanger ram air intake
35 Electrical system circuit breaker panels, port and starboard
36 Avionics equipment
37 Avionics bay access doors, port and starboard
38 Formation-keeping luminous strip
39 Ventral airbrake
40 Airbrake hydraulic jack
41 Avionics equipment racks
42 Fuselage frame and stringer construction
43 Rear fuselage fuel tank
44 Main undercarriage wheelbay
45 Wing-root fillet
46 Wing spar/fuselage attachment joint
47 Water filler cap
48 Engine fire extinguisher bottle
49 Anti-collision light
50 Fuel tank
51 Flap hydraulic actuator
52 Flap hinge fitting
53 Nimonic fuselage heat shield
54 Main undercarriage bay doors (closed after cycling of undercarriage)
55 Flap vane composite construction
56 Flap composite construction
57 Starboard slotted flap, lowered

58 Outrigger wheel fairing
59 Outrigger leg doors
60 Starboard aileron
61 Aileron composite construction
62 Fuel jettison
63 Formation lights
64 Roll control air valve
65 Wing-tip fairing
66 Starboard/forward missile warning radar antenna
67 Starboard navigation light
68 Radar warning antenna
69 540 lb (245 kg) low drag HE bomb (retarded version, alternative)
70 Outboard pylon
71 Pylon attachment joint
72 Graphite epoxy composite wing construction
73 Aileron hydraulic actuator
74 Starboard outrigger wheel
75 2.75 in (70 mm) HVAR folding fin rocket
76 Matra 155 rocket launcher (18 rockets)
77 Intermediate pylon
78 Pylon attachment joint
79 Reaction control air ducting
80 Chaff/flare dispensers each side of missile pylon
81 Aileron control rod
82 Outrigger hydraulic retraction jack
83 Outrigger leg strut
84 Leg pivot fixing
85 Multi-spar wing construction
86 Leading-edge wing fence
87 Outrigger pylon
88 Missile launch rail
89 AIM-9L Sidewinder air-to-air missile
90 1000 lb (454 kg) retarded HE bomb (free-fall version, alternative)
91 External fuel tank, 300 US gal (250 Imp gal/1351 l)
92 Inboard pylon
93 Aft retracting mainwheels

94 Inboard pylon attachment joint
95 Rear (hot steam) swivelling exhaust nozzle
96 Position of pressure refuelling connection on port side
97 Rear nozzle bearing
98 Centre fuselage flank fuel tank
99 Hydraulic reservoir
100 Nozzle bearing cooling air duct
101 Engine exhaust divider duct
102 Wing panel centre rib
103 Centre section integral fuel tank
104 Port wing integral fuel tank
105 Flap vane
106 Port slotted flap, lowered
107 Outrigger wheel fairing
108 Port outrigger wheel
109 Torque scissor links
110 Port aileron
111 Aileron hydraulic actuator
112 Aileron/air valve interconnection
113 Fuel jettison
114 Formation lights
115 Port roll control air valve
116 Port/forward missile warning radar antenna

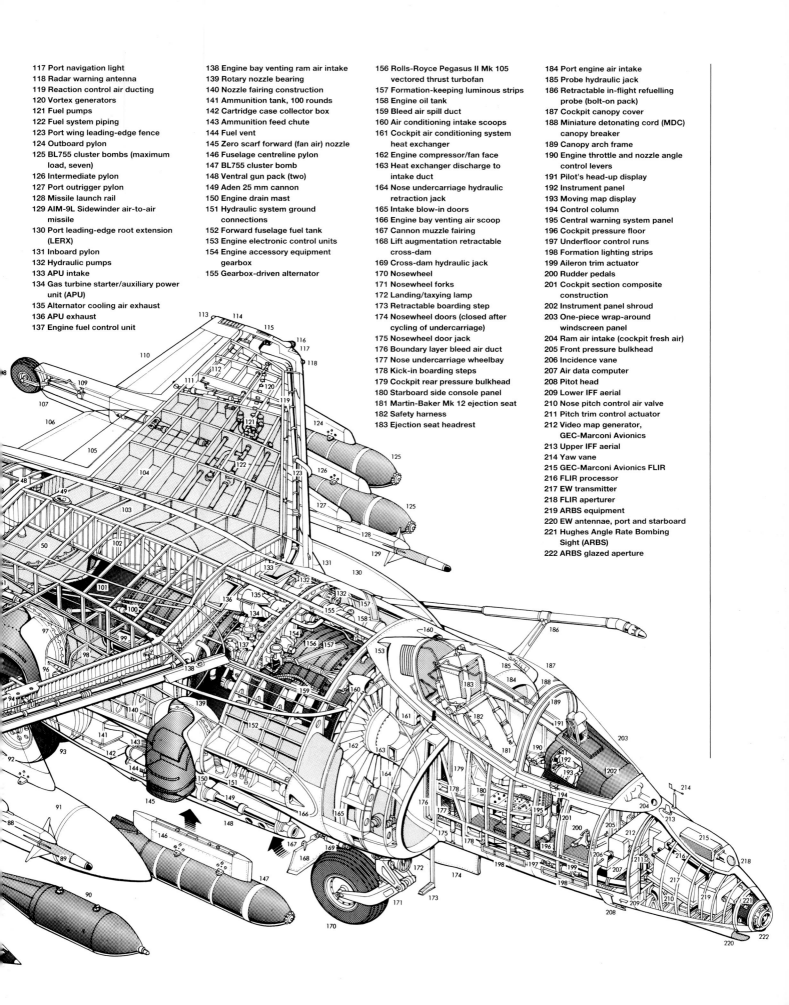

117 Port navigation light
118 Radar warning antenna
119 Reaction control air ducting
120 Vortex generators
121 Fuel pumps
122 Fuel system piping
123 Port wing leading-edge fence
124 Outboard pylon
125 BL755 cluster bombs (maximum load, seven)
126 Intermediate pylon
127 Port outrigger pylon
128 Missile launch rail
129 AIM-9L Sidewinder air-to-air missile
130 Port leading-edge root extension (LERX)
131 Inboard pylon
132 Hydraulic pumps
133 APU intake
134 Gas turbine starter/auxiliary power unit (APU)
135 Alternator cooling air exhaust
136 APU exhaust
137 Engine fuel control unit

138 Engine bay venting ram air intake
139 Rotary nozzle bearing
140 Nozzle fairing construction
141 Ammunition tank, 100 rounds
142 Cartridge case collector box
143 Ammunition feed chute
144 Fuel vent
145 Zero scarf forward (fan air) nozzle
146 Fuselage centreline pylon
147 BL755 cluster bomb
148 Ventral gun pack (two)
149 Aden 25 mm cannon
150 Engine drain mast
151 Hydraulic system ground connections
152 Forward fuselage fuel tank
153 Engine electronic control units
154 Engine accessory equipment gearbox
155 Gearbox-driven alternator

156 Rolls-Royce Pegasus II Mk 105 vectored thrust turbofan
157 Formation-keeping luminous strips
158 Engine oil tank
159 Bleed air spill duct
160 Air conditioning intake scoops
161 Cockpit air conditioning system heat exchanger
162 Engine compressor/fan face
163 Heat exchanger discharge to intake duct
164 Nose undercarriage hydraulic retraction jack
165 Intake blow-in doors
166 Engine bay venting air scoop
167 Cannon muzzle fairing
168 Lift augmentation retractable cross-dam
169 Cross-dam hydraulic jack
170 Nosewheel
171 Nosewheel forks
172 Landing/taxiing lamp
173 Retractable boarding step
174 Nosewheel doors (closed after cycling of undercarriage)
175 Nosewheel door jack
176 Boundary layer bleed air duct
177 Nose undercarriage wheelbay
178 Kick-in boarding steps
179 Cockpit rear pressure bulkhead
180 Starboard side console panel
181 Martin-Baker Mk 12 ejection seat
182 Safety harness
183 Ejection seat headrest

184 Port engine air intake
185 Probe hydraulic jack
186 Retractable in-flight refuelling probe (bolt-on pack)
187 Cockpit canopy cover
188 Miniature detonating cord (MDC) canopy breaker
189 Canopy arch frame
190 Engine throttle and nozzle angle control levers
191 Pilot's head-up display
192 Instrument panel
193 Moving map display
194 Control column
195 Central warning system panel
196 Cockpit pressure floor
197 Underfloor control runs
198 Formation lighting strips
199 Aileron trim actuator
200 Rudder pedals
201 Cockpit section composite construction
202 Instrument panel shroud
203 One-piece wrap-around windscreen panel
204 Ram air intake (cockpit fresh air)
205 Front pressure bulkhead
206 Incidence vane
207 Air data computer
208 Pitot head
209 Lower IFF aerial
210 Nose pitch control air valve
211 Pitch trim control actuator
212 Video map generator, GEC-Marconi Avionics
213 Upper IFF aerial
214 Yaw vane
215 GEC-Marconi Avionics FLIR
216 FLIR processor
217 EW transmitter
218 FLIR aperturer
219 ARBS equipment
220 EW antennae, port and starboard
221 Hughes Angle Rate Bombing Sight (ARBS)
222 ARBS glazed aperture

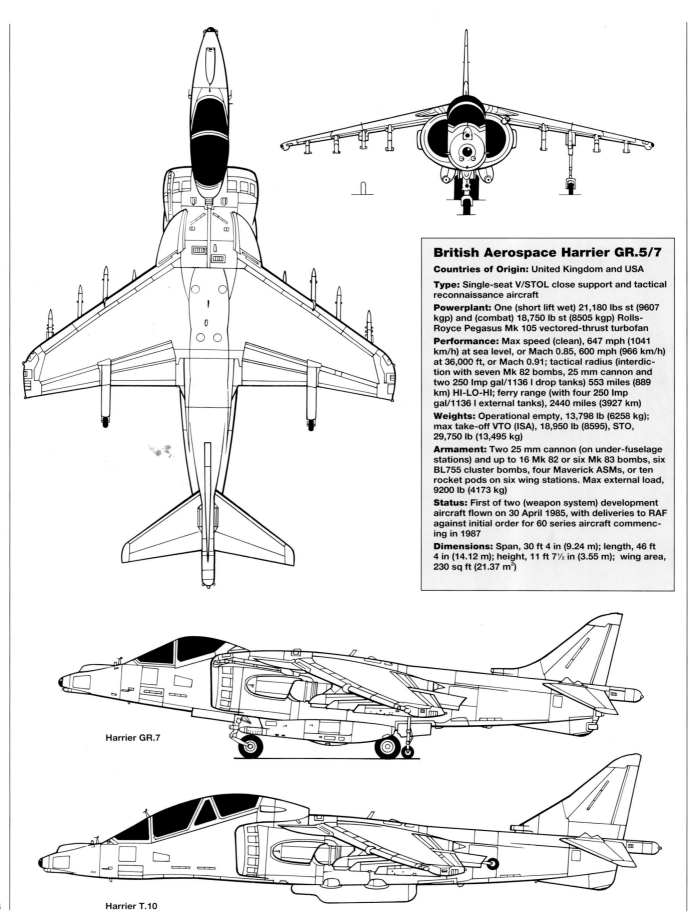

British Aerospace Harrier GR.5/7

Countries of Origin: United Kingdom and USA

Type: Single-seat V/STOL close support and tactical reconnaissance aircraft

Powerplant: One (short lift wet) 21,180 lbs st (9607 kgp) and (combat) 18,750 lb st (8505 kgp) Rolls-Royce Pegasus Mk 105 vectored-thrust turbofan

Performance: Max speed (clean), 647 mph (1041 km/h) at sea level, or Mach 0.85, 600 mph (966 km/h) at 36,000 ft, or Mach 0.91; tactical radius (interdiction with seven Mk 82 bombs, 25 mm cannon and two 250 Imp gal/1136 l drop tanks) 553 miles (889 km) HI-LO-HI; ferry range (with four 250 Imp gal/1136 l external tanks), 2440 miles (3927 km)

Weights: Operational empty, 13,798 lb (6258 kg); max take-off VTO (ISA), 18,950 lb (8595), STO, 29,750 lb (13,495 kg)

Armament: Two 25 mm cannon (on under-fuselage stations) and up to 16 Mk 82 or six Mk 83 bombs, six BL755 cluster bombs, four Maverick ASMs, or ten rocket pods on six wing stations. Max external load, 9200 lb (4173 kg)

Status: First of two (weapon system) development aircraft flown on 30 April 1985, with deliveries to RAF against initial order for 60 series aircraft commencing in 1987

Dimensions: Span, 30 ft 4 in (9.24 m); length, 46 ft 4 in (14.12 m); height, 11 ft 7½ in (3.55 m); wing area, 230 sq ft (21.37 m²)

Harrier GR.7

Harrier T.10